The Management of Small

HISTORY MUSEUMS

Carl E. Guthe

Second Edition

The American Association for State and Local History
Nashville

Second edition, third printing 1974
Second edition, fourth printing 1977
ISBN 0-910050-04-X

Typography, Printing, and Binding in the U.S.A. by
Williams Printing Company, Nashville, Tennessee

Preface to the Second Edition

Five years ago Albert B. Corey, the late and beloved State Historian of New York, noted in his preface to the first edition of this work that it marked a milestone in museum literature. How truly he spoke has been demonstrated amply by the unceasing demand for a volume that has earned a much deserved place on the shelf of "must" reading for historical administrators. Through its pages untold numbers of historical museums and historic sites have learned to do a better and more effective job for the vast public they serve. Its contribution to the raising of standards in these museums and sites is incalculable.

The American Association for State and Local History is proud to have had the privilege of first issuing Carl Guthe's work as the tenth number of the second volume of its now concluded bulletin series. It is with both pride and gratification that we respond to the heavy demand for this book by publishing this second edition. This new volume has been redesigned, the type completely reset, and a few minor changes made in front matter and text. With these exceptions, however, the present book is the same as the slender predecessor that in a few short years has become a classic for the guidance of those who through their historical societies, sites, and museums seek to preserve and interpret the American experience.

WILLIAM T. ALDERSON, JR.
Nashville, Tennessee

Preface

The publication of this manual marks an especially significant milestone in museum literature. For the first time the history museum, and in particular the small history museum, is singled out as the institution that needs professionalization on the one hand and historical perspective on the other. The importance of this book can therefore hardly be over-estimated.

Too many small history museums still belie the name of museum. Many are little more than depositories of historical objects. Their collections are not adequately cataloged or are not cataloged at all. Their methods of preservation do credit to attic storehouses. Their exhibits are little more than organized confusion. Too often they are proud to own relics that are meaningful only to them and a small body of associates. Articles are exhibited because of their sentimental value to the few or to donors, not because they illumine the human processes of the past.

Fortunately, much has been done in the last two-score years to define, establish, and encourage better museum practices. Among the leaders in this movement, no one knows the museum field better than Carl Guthe, who, after retiring as director of the New York State Museum, spent five years visiting museums of every description throughout the United States and Canada.

Many a small museum in New York State is profiting from his personal touch; hundreds elsewhere have received the benefit of his wide knowledge, experience, and advice. It is from the wealth of such background that he has written the present volume.

The key to an understanding of the history museum is best expressed in Dr. Guthe's own words: "The exhibit program in each history museum," he says, "differs from that in every other because it reflects the significant experiences of the community it serves and the attitudes and policies of the citizens who direct its destinies." This statement should be engraved upon the memories of all small history museum personnel.

There is one thing that this manual *cannot* do for the director or other head of the small history museum. Although it gives him procedural and technical advice and encouragement to carry forward a good program, and an understanding of most of the problems that he is likely to meet, it cannot help him to develop a stimulating museum program unless he has a good working knowledge of historical processes, a capacity for painstaking effort, and an artistic imagination with which to capture the spirit of the past and make it live in meaningful exhibits. These things a man must acquire for himself.

Historical societies are increasingly and very properly widening their perspective and their programs to encompass the story of the many and varied activities of men. To the task of colorful, stimulating, and thoughtful interpretation of the past they are bringing many disciplines to bear with telling effect. Among these are the newer media of communication and the age-old medium of display and description so well explained in this book. The better that historical museum personnel learn proper museum techniques, the more effective will be the contribution of historical societies to the past they seek to illuminate.

The American Association for State and Local History is indeed fortunate to publish this manual, which will be so useful to so many persons who look forward to creating imaginative small history museums.

ALBERT B. COREY
Albany, New York

Contents

General Considerations

Interest in historical subjects has been increasing rapidly throughout the country in recent years. It has been attributed to growing maturity of our society. It has been explained as one of the results of the increase of leisure and the expansion of travel. Certainly a contributing factor is the development of new and attractive ways of stimulating this interest.

Books and documents, which have traditionally served as the principal source of historical information, now share this growing interest with a wide variety of other media of communication. Radio and television have joined with the older medium, the motion pictures, in bringing life, action, and excitement to history. Tourist attractions, capitalizing on regional history, and catering to the entertainment and curiosity of the traveling public, are widely distributed. Unfortunately, these agencies are often primarily sources of entertainment in which no clear distinction is drawn between fact and fiction.

On the other hand, responsible scholar and educational organizations, devoted to the accurate and truthful interpretation of history, also sponsor new and often exciting ways of stimulating public interest in our heritage. Anniversaries, centennials, and semicentennials of important dates being celebrated in many localities serve as foci for the review of past group experiences.

Pageants and outdoor dramas, sometimes of several days' duration, enable spectators to relive vicariously thrilling historic episodes. For more than a century it has been the custom to protect as historical memorials various buildings, battlefields, and similar sites associated with outstanding past achievements. The tremendous expansion of automotive travel has resulted in the rapid increase and sound improvement of these historic landmarks.

Closely related to this program of protecting and preserving the integrity of restricted sites and structures is the relatively recent development of the concept of recreating an entire community of an historical period, of which Colonial Williamsburg is the most famous and elaborate example. There are dozens of these historic communities throughout the country, in which the visitor is given the opportunity to step back, as it were, into an earlier way of life.

These historic villages, houses, and sites, and pageants, dramas, and celebrations attract tens of millions of visitors each year. This popularity lies not in their amusing old-fashioned quaintness, but rather in their inspiring historical authenticity in every detail. The responsive visitors sense at once the validity of these excursions into the living past.

An old and respected institution which is widely used to encourage the growing interest in historical matters is the museum. Its distinctive quality is that it brings the visitor into direct contact with the tangible objects that were a part of the events, the customs, and the conditions of former years. A history museum is an institution dedicated to the preservation and interpretation of collections of significant historic objects. In the broad sense, historic houses and villages and other sites are forms of museums because they involve the use and preservation of tangible objects. In fact the historic villages are sometimes called out-door, or living, museums. In the stricter sense, however, the term history museum refers to the institution that assembles, preserves, and interprets the smaller movable objects which have historical meaning.

There are many kinds of history museums. Some are independent corporations. Others are units of larger organizations which have more diversified or broader interests. The federal and state governments maintain history museums; so do city, town and county governments. Educational institutions, industrial corporations, professional associations and many other societies frequently operate historical museums as part of their activities.

The nature of the collections that the history museum assembles depends upon the historical interests of the organization of which it is a part. There are museums devoted to interpreting the story of the development of the fur trade, of the glass industry, of photography, of World War II, of the automobile, of money, of horse racing, and of many more specific subjects such as battles, inventions, and dramatic incidents. No two museums are alike, for the character of each inevitably reflects the attitudes, policies, and objectives of its sponsoring organization.

The majority of history museums, however, are those concerned with the story of a restricted geographical area. There are of course the historical collections in the many museums operated by state governments. But these are far outnumbered by small local museums dealing with the history of cities, towns, or counties, which are operated by museum commissions of city or county governments, by city libraries, by park boards, or by local historical societies.

About sixty percent of the 1821 museums surveyed by the National Endowment for the Arts in 1972 had historical collections. Nearly 700 were exclusively or predominantly history. Many small museums were excluded from the survey because budgets, staff, and visiting hours were too limited to meet the guidelines of the survey. Had they been included history museums would have accounted for half or more of the entire museum field. Thus small history museums, even though they are sometimes the "poor relations" of the profession, and important both for their numbers and because they are frequently the only museums in their communities. The character of the entire museum movement is likely to be judged locally by their achievements.

The dedicated groups of citizens who sponsor local history museums are well aware of what they wish to accomplish, but in the majority of instances they find it difficult to work out the practical and most effective ways and means of achieving these ends. They are entitled to a knowledge of the generally accepted principles under which the larger and the successful museums operate, as a means of helping and guiding them in their own undertakings.

The purpose of this bulletin is to make available to the small history museum the fundamentals of good museum operation.

The procedures which have been found to be successful, as well as the reasoning which has led to their wide acceptance, are discussed in the hope that thereby officials of the small museums will be stimulated to interpret and adapt the recommended practices to the conditions and situations governing their individual opportunities.

PHYSICAL FACILITIES

Before discussing the collections and their interpretation, some attention should be given to the manner in which the museum is housed and the problem of the responsibility for the museum. Small museums either have apparently adequate quarters, are anticipating moving into more suitable accommodations, or, when newly organized, are seeking satisfactory housing. It is advisable to review the suitability of available quarters in terms of security, accessibility, space requirements, capital outlay, and maintenance costs.

The primary consideration is one of security. The museum's principal capital assets are its collections. Every practical safeguard against their loss and deterioration should be adopted. The museum building must be of sound construction and should be as nearly fire-resistant as is practical. The danger of unauthorized entry and the cost of insurance premiums may be reduced by having as few doors as possible, each of which can be locked securely. It is inadvisable to use a wooden frame building, in spite of the fact that many small museums are so housed. The factor of security should never be compromised for the sake of securing quarters that are otherwise attractive.

One of the functions of the museum is to render public service. It should therefore be easily accessible to visitors—to the local citizens who are moving about on other business; to the school classes who desire to visit the exhibits; and to transients seeking local information. The center of town is a convenient location, easily accessible to the greatest number of potential visitors. Its disadvantages are the restricted available space, the impossibility of future expansion, and the lack of adequate parking facilities. An attractive location is in a residential area relatively near the center of town. It is adjacent to main arteries of traffic and can be reached easily by city bus or streetcar. If the building is surrounded by landscaped grounds, parking space can be prepared. However, the museum should not be located in an underprivileged area where vandalism may occur, or in an area that people prefer to avoid in the evenings. When the community is developing a civic center, it is most appropriate to include the museum as one of the buildings in the complex. Another alternative is to locate the museum near the edge of town, preferably in a popular city park. Here the museum enjoys pleasing surroundings, and can afford plenty of parking space for visitors. The drawbacks to such a location are the greater time and effort required to reach it by car or by public conveyance, and its relative isolation during the evenings and in inclement weather. There is also greater danger of molestation and vandalism.

The amount of floor space needed by the museum is probably the determining consideration in the choice of suitable quarters. The number of square feet needed should not be determined casually. Several factors must be recognized and evaluated. The size of the collections bears a direct relationship to the amount of floor space used. In an active museum the collections will increase steadily and may even double in size in a ten-year period. Adequate provision for such expansion should be made in reaching an estimate of the amount of floor space the museum will require.

The primary obligation of a museum is to assemble and preserve its collections. The articles must be put somewhere when they are first received. They must then be sorted and inspected to determine the need for cleaning and repairing. Complete records must be made on all of them. There must be room in which to keep in a safe and orderly way the materials not used in the exhibit halls. All these essential activities require floor space.

A serious error is to estimate space requirements solely in terms of public exhibit halls. This is a natural mistake, for the great majority of visitors see only the exhibit halls and do not visit the other rooms of the institution, where most of the daily activities are performed. It is often assumed that a museum needs only sufficient room to display in glass cases all of the materials in its collections. This lack of distinction between the exhibits and the collections results in crowded display cases, a prodigal and inefficient use of floor space, and an early demand for expansion of quarters.

The public exhibit rooms of the museum are analogous to the public reading rooms of a library. The books most frequently needed by library visitors are kept on the reference shelves in the reading room. Most of the items in the library collections are filed in the stacks, in an orderly manner so that they may be located easily when called for. The same system is used in a well-organized museum. The objects from the collections that are of most interest to visitors are on display in the exhibit halls. One-half to three-quarters or more of the materials in the collections are kept in drawers and cabinets in the collection files, not open to the general public, though they are to students and scholars. Here they are arranged in an orderly and compact fashion which makes it possible to find any item easily and quickly when it is needed.

A generally recognized rule-of-thumb formula for museum space assignment calls for devoting approximately forty percent of floor space to public exhibit halls, another forty percent to collection filing rooms and associated work rooms and laboratories, and the remaining twenty percent to staff offices and service and maintenance rooms.

A fortunate small history museum may be occupying an old mansion, having a total floor space of about 3,000 square feet, the equivalent of ten rooms each 15 by 20 feet in size. The most efficient use of these quarters would call for assigning four or five rooms on the first floor, the equivalent of 1,200 to 1,500 square feet, to the public exhibits, and devoting the remainder to the other museum requirements. If the only available quarters are one or two rooms in a public building and total only 1,000 square feet of floor space, then it is advisable to devote not more than fifty percent of the space, an area 25 by 20 feet in size, to public displays.

Many people may be shocked by these recommendations and insist that they cannot be applied to their museums. It is true that very few small museums, even those that do possess collection filing and work rooms, approximate these recommended space assignments. Yet the museums that have restricted exhibit halls, and possess ample space for processing, studying, and filing their collections, are among those that most successfully meet museum standards and obligations.

These recommendations should not be dismissed as impractical without careful consideration. Their reasonableness will become more apparent later, as various museum practices are discussed. Their adoption may require a radical change in policy. Two basic principles need to be remembered: the primary obligation of a museum is to guarantee adequate preservation of the collections and effective use of their contents; and the success of an exhibit program is established by attractive and stimulating displays, not by the size of the public exhibit halls, the number of glass cases, or the quantity of individual items shown.

The two remaining considerations in the choice of a home for the museum are financial in character, namely, the capital outlay required and the annual maintenance costs. In a very few instances, small history museums have been fortunate in being able to plan and construct their own buildings, thanks to the generosity of their friends. The overwhelming majority secure quarters for their collections either as gifts or on nominal leases. Museum property is usually tax free because it is occupied by a non-profit educational institution rendering public service.

A museum may have the opportunity to acquire an old residence, public garage, store, or a vacant public building or school. The nature of the use to which the property had formerly been put is of no significance, provided it is structurally sound and meets the requirements of security, accessibility, and usable space. In the case of former residences it is well to investigate the status of liens, such as mortgages and tax claims on the property.

Before deciding to acquire any building, an architect or a contractor, or both, should be employed to determine the nature and extent of any repairs that need to be made, and of any alterations required to adapt the structure to museum use. The cost of such work is, of course, a capital expense. Similarly, the cost of any new equipment for the exhibit halls, the filing rooms, offices, and laboratories is capital expense. Obviously, before assuming responsibility for the property, the museum organization must be sure this investment can be met by arrangement with the former owners, through contributed services, through financial grants, or out of its own capital.

The annual cost of maintenance of the property should be estimated before acquiring it. The greater probable frequency of needed repairs in older buildings may increase this expense. The cost of heating and the charges for public utilities and telephone must be included. The expense of employing permanent and seasonal labor to keep the building and grounds in continuously good condition may be considerable. A museum occupying a few rooms, or all of the space, in public buildings may have low maintenance expenses, because the city or county government assumes responsibility for the maintenance of the property, with the exception, perhaps, of some janitorial services. Normal maintenance costs should involve only a reasonably small proportion of the annual income of the museum. They should not unduly restrict the funds for normal operation and expansion.

ORGANIZATION

The museum being safely housed, it is now necessary to determine who should be responsible for it. Every formal organization is controlled by a group of responsible citizens, generally known as a board of some kind, which is legally responsible for its organization, its activities, and its commitments. The actual management of the organization is delegated by the board to an administrator and his staff.

A small history museum, in order to hold property and handle funds, must be a formally recognized organization governed by a controlling board which is legally responsible for its economic integrity, ethical conduct, and operating policies. If the museum is an independent corporation, it has its own board of trustees. If it is a city or county agency, the controlling board is either the city council or the county board of supervisors or commissioners. If it is sponsored by a society or association, it is governed by the board of directors of the sponsoring organization. If it is a unit of an educational institution or of an industrial corporation, its controlling board is the governing body of the parent organization.

When the museum is a part of a larger organization, the actual body in control of the museum is likely to be a subsidiary of the legally responsible board. Under governmental control it may be a city or county museum commission, a city or county park commission, or a library or school board. The breakdown may proceed still further to a museum committee of the library or school board. Under private control, authority is usually delegated to a museum committee, one of the standing committees of the parent board. The reason for this delegation of authority is that the legally responsible board has multiple responsibilities, the performance of which prevents it from devoting sufficient time to the consideration of museum business. It must therefore delegate this responsibility to a standing committee in which are vested all of the prerogatives and responsibilities of the parent board, and which reports its decisions and actions back to the board.

The organizational pattern by which the museum board acquires its title and its delegated authority may be simple or complex, but its functions in relation to the museum are always the same. Whether the board in control is the board of trustees of the museum corporation, the museum committee of the board of county supervisors, or the board of trustees of the local historical society, its members are responsible, as trustees for the people, for the museum's economic stability, good name, and management policies.

The governing board is usually composed of a small number of substantial citizens who are interested in the museum and have accepted the responsibilities implicit in their membership. Some of them are members of other similar boards. All of them devote most of their time and energy to their individual vocations or avocations. They can afford to give relatively little time to museum affairs. They are on the board in order to contribute their knowledge and wisdom to the discussion and formulation of wise and practical policies controlling the museum's destinies. They are entitled to full information on all subjects requiring decisions, and to reports upon the results achieved by those decisions. And here their duties and responsibilities end. The museum board is a legislative and policy forming board, not an administrative one.

This is as it should be. The board members are admittedly not trained in museum work. They do not have the time to familiarize themselves with the interacting needs, crises, and objectives relating to any incident they may encounter during a visit to the museum. They should not give orders directly to museum workers and should furnish advice only when it is requested. Apparent divided authority weakens effective performance. The individual board member should not officially express personal opinions concerning the management of the museum except at formal meetings of the board.

That being the case, how is the museum run? Normally the board will appoint someone to carry out its policies and administer the daily activities of the museum. This person, with the title "director," should be salaried and devote his full time to the museum. The incumbent should be a college graduate with an adequate knowledge of history and of museum practices. In order to maintain the dignity of the museum and to attract the right kind of person, the salary offered the director of a small history museum should be commensurate with that of a principal in the city's school system, or that of the head of a similar city agency, such as the public library. The employment of additional staff members depends entirely upon the museum's finances. In most cases about two-thirds of the annual income is spent on payroll.

Some small museums do not have incomes sufficient to employ a full-time competent staff member. A possible compromise is to employ a part-time attendant, with the title "custodian" or "hostess," for the exhibit rooms while they are open to the public. He or she should be someone who likes people, is well informed on local history and on the materials in the collections, is able to greet the visitors pleasantly, and can make them feel at home. It is advisable to avoid securing some garrulous individual inclined to recount vivid and inaccurate stories about the items in the collections. One further note of caution: it is shortsighted to offer an unattractively low hourly pay rate for such services. The presence of an uninformed custodian or hostess, obviously assigned to the exhibit hall to guard against vandalism and theft, discourages visitors.

A part-time custodian or hostess is equivalent to a clerk, and usually cannot be given administrative authority. If this is the only staff member the museum can afford, then its management must be vested in some volunteer who has the enthusiasm, ability, time, and energy to assume the responsibilities for its administration and who can be held accountable for the actions taken. The direction of the work of the museum should not be assigned to a committee. Misunderstandings, disagreements on procedures, and personality conflicts are bound to result, and the museum will be the principal victim.

Various methods are used to relate the volunteer administrator to the organization. Sometimes the president of the society or the association, or the chairman of the governing board, is assigned these additional duties. Or it may be the chairman of the museum committee who is given the job. In other instances the volunteer is given the title "curator" or "honorary curator" and is elected either a full member or an ex-officio member of the governing board. It matters not how it is accomplished providing the volunteer receives a due measure of prestige as well as appreciation for the responsibilities that have been assumed.

The small museum that is unable to pay any wages is bound to have difficulties. All the work with the collections or in the exhibits and with visiting school classes must then be done by volunteers. As individuals they will be able to help at the museum for only a few hours one or two days a week. The work will be done inefficiently and progress will be exasperatingly slow. Sometimes the organized volunteer services of the Junior League, the American Association of University Women, or similar groups are used. It has been found that the most effective services are secured by persuading the volunteers to organize themselves as a museum "auxiliary" or "guild."

The organized museum volunteers will have their own governing board, officers, and committees. They will be able to take responsibility for scheduling the tours of duty of the members and, through committees, secure replacements for unavoidable absences. Under the guidance of the administrator, they can make a survey of the types of work needed in the museum and establish committees to carry out these projects.

The volunteer administrator of a very small museum should not be a member of the organized volunteer group, but should act as the museum staff member who guides and directs the work. The volunteer services of members of an organized museum auxiliary are being used successfully by many large and small museums.

Every community has individuals with special talents and interests which can be used advantageously by history museums. These persons, when approached by museum officials, will feel honored by the recognition of their abilities and usually will offer their services on a volunteer basis. It is customary to ask bankers and lawyers to serve on the governing board, where their knowledge and experience prove most valuable. Artists and designers can make substantial contributions to the planning and installation of exhibits. Those who pursue handicraft hobbies, such as needle work, carpentry, and metal working, can render valuable assistance in the maintenance of the collections and in the construction and repair of equipment. Model enthusiasts can become interested in creating scale miniatures of historical objects by following specifications of the originals. Collectors of one or more classes of historical objects, such as furniture, firearms, glassware, china, and similar materials, may have acquired a technical knowledge which is valuable in identifying and evaluating objects in the collections. Retired persons, including "retired" mothers whose children are sufficiently grown to no longer need their constant attention, may be persuaded to contribute their free time and their talents to advancing the museum program. These are merely illustrations of the many ways in which individual citizens with special aptitudes may identify themselves with the history museum and its activities.

This type of volunteer work differs from that of the museum "auxiliary" or "guild" in that it is highly individualized. The amount of time each person devotes to museum work is determined by his interest, and the degree of responsibility assigned him depends upon his special qualifications. Appropriate recognition needs to be given these volunteers. They may be listed officially as "collaborators," "honorary curators," "research associates," or "museum aids."

Every museum should seek out those citizens who possess talents, interests or hobbies that are related to its program. By enlisting their active participation in the work of the museum, its development will be more rapid, the number of persons identifying themselves with its program will increase, and its integration into the daily life of the community will be strengthened.

The Collections

A museum is judged by its collections. Their possession accounts for its existence; their character determines its worth. Just as the quality of the holdings of an investment portfolio reflects the judgment and planning of its owner, so also the character of the holdings in the collections reveals the policies and objectives of the museum. The nature and the scope of the collections should be considered and defined by the board responsible for the museum.

Many a history museum has been started by pooling the private collections of several of its founders. In the beginning it seems to be natural to consider the museum as a custodian and holding company for a series of private collections, through which they become accessible to a wider interested public. In time the identity of the separate collections is weakened. The museum officers treat the combined collections as the property of the institution, the contents of which they generously display for the benefit of visitors to the museum's exhibit halls. They have failed to recognize the gradual change in the status of the collections.

A museum that professes to be a public institution thereby recognizes that its existence depends upon the good will of the community. It matters not whether it is subsidized by tax funds or supported by the income of a private non-profit educational corporation. Its management practices and its business procedures must have public approval. This applies also to its principal assets, the collections. Their legal ownership may be vested in the governing board. The members of that board act as trustees of the museum for the people. The collections, the core of the institution, fall under this trusteeship. They have lost their private nature; their management is no longer the private prerogative of the museum and its officials. The collections have become a public heritage held in trust by the museum for the benefit of the present and future citizens of the community. This transition of the collections from private property to a public trust needs to be recognized fully in formulating the policies and establishing the objectives of the small history museum.

It is equally important to establish the scope of the collections. A disregard of the need for setting limitations upon the subjects dealt with in the collections may result in the accumulation of a much too diversified and fruitless miscellany of objects. It seems reasonable to expect a museum's collections to conform with its objectives. A hardware store does not usually sell furniture. As a rule the small history museum is concerned with the story of a city, town, county, or restricted geographical area. Surely its collections should be circumscribed by the purpose of the museum. If its interests are limited to a particular industry, activity, or historic incident or period, the material in the collections should, logically, deal only with the special historical fields.

Limiting the scope of the museum's collections to relevant historical materials seems to be a sound and reasonable policy. Yet a small history museum is most frequently the only museum in a community. Traditionally a museum has been expected to display interesting and unusual things. It will be offered all manner of objects that individual citizens consider worth saving. The museums' board will be forced to resolve the very practical dilemma of choosing between the acceptance or refusal of such gifts.

Collectors in the community may have acquired groups of porcelains, glassware, coins, stamps, or salt and pepper shakers. Local amateur scientists may have assembled scientific and natural history specimens—mounted birds, egg collections, minerals, Indian relics, or shells from the Florida beaches. Other citizens may have accumulated as souvenirs examples of the arts and crafts of distant lands. All of these have three things in common:

first, their present owners will sooner or later wish to dispose of them; second, each or all of them will be offered to the museum as gifts; and third, none of them are relevant to the local history with which the museum is primarily concerned.

Occasionally there are reasonable arguments for not limiting the scope of the collections too strictly. If the museum already possesses fine collections of such irrelevant materials, it is certainly much easier to accept the fact as a necessary complication than it is to undertake negotiations for their disposal. Articles from foreign lands and natural history specimens may be of great interest to some visitors because of their technical significance, their aesthetic quality, their intrinsic worth, or their representation of expert craftsmanship, and should be preserved. These private collections are the tangible results of many hours of patient search and study, and often represent substantial financial investments. To allow the items to become widely scattered would destroy the effect of years of collecting and diminish their comparative study value. In small and young museums such materials would add to the attractiveness of, and help fill, the glass cases in the exhibit halls. They may have definite educational value in the instruction given visiting school classes. However, the retention of materials that lie outside the museum's purpose should not be treated lightly.

There are good reasons for not accepting materials that are irrelevant to the major interests of the museum. A careless collecting policy may cause it to become an overcrowded repository for miscellaneous discarded materials, a sort of community attic. Objects directly connected with the story of the community should appeal to a greater number of visitors. Every observer tends to be interested in those that relate in some way to his own knowledge, experience, and needs. The native citizen will impart a deeper meaning to materials associated with the story of his community and the life of his forebears. The recent arrivals and the tourists will find in these historical items the key to a better understanding of the community. Responsible citizens may well question the sincerity and good judgment of those in charge of a local museum that collects and displays interesting and unusual articles having no connection whatever with the story of the community, the interpretation of which is the ostensible reason for the museum's existence. These irrelevant objects in the collections take up shelf space in the filing rooms and display space in the exhibit halls which should be occupied with materials relating to the local history. As for school classes, the lessons taught by displays interpreting the growth of the community will have more lasting value than those derived from objects only remotely associated with their own experiences.

The decision establishing the scope of the museum's collections is probably the most important one that the governing board can make. It will determine the future variety of their contents and thereby dictate the character of the institution. It is also a difficult decision. The board will be required to evaluate objectively the conflicting arguments advanced by various pressure groups, each of which will represent a relatively small, but possibly influential, segment of the public. Strong differences of opinion may exist even within the board's membership. The museum board, as the trustee for the community, will ultimately reach a majority decision, defining the type of collections which, in its best judgment, will most effectively meet the present and future interests and needs of the community as a whole.

In the small museums which are just being established this vital decision is relatively easy because it relates only to the future. In others the decision may already have been made and requires only a thoughtful re-analysis, with the possible strengthening of certain conditions of the policies derived from it. In a great many small museums, however, no serious attention has ever been given to limiting the scope of the collections. Holdings frequently consist of a variety of articles reflecting the catholic interests of the founder of, and principal donor to, the museum, to which have been added other materials that seemed to be worth keeping when they were offered. It is this last group of museums in which the proper decision will be most difficult to achieve. Three possible types of action can be taken.

The first of these is to follow the path of least resistance. When there is only one museum in the community, it may seem advisable to maintain general collections of interesting, attractive, and unusual objects not found in most homes. By displaying these for the education and entertainment of visitors, the museum may be said to be meeting the widely diversified interests and needs of the greatest number of citizens in the community.

Since general collections will grow rapidly in size, adequate provisions must exist for the physical handling and filing of these materials, and the staff must be large enough to insure their proper maintenance. Unless the museum consistently renders interesting and useful services, it may soon become an attractive but unessential element in the life of the community. If the museum's legal and official purpose is the preservation and interpretation of historical materials, then the possession of general miscellaneous collections may confuse the public concerning its objectives and bring about a gradually increasing loss of public interest and support. This is particularly likely to occur if the character of the collections contradicts the title of the institution. General collections are inappropriate in the "Smith County Historical Society Museum."

An alternative action may be advisable when social pressure is so strong that the museum is forced to accept collections of miscellaneous objects in order to preserve them. Such action can be taken under protest, pointing out that the materials do not fall within the previously determined scope of the museum's collections and that their housing and care require space and energy which should be devoted more profitably to the historical collections of the institution. It should be made clear that these collections would be kept in the filing room and would receive the minimum amount of attention necessary for their preservation. The museum would agree to act as custodian only until a more appropriate depository for them could be found.

The adoption of this expedient policy in a small museum already possessing general miscellaneous collections would logically call for a drastic change in the exhibit program. The materials and subjects within the scope of the institution's objectives should dominate that program. Those irrelevant to these objectives should be withdrawn from display and stored in the collection files. If space and time permitted, small portions of these could be used for short periods in temporary and special exhibitions. This type of action involves considerable work and will invite criticism, but should contribute to a better understanding of the museum's objectives and increase its prestige as a public service institution.

The third and wisest course of action is to make the uncompromising decision that the scope of the collections shall be limited to materials directly related to the museum's objectives. This is the policy usually followed by specialized history museums concerned with the growth of a particular industry, the development of a social activity, or the interpretation of an important historic episode. A small local history museum should restrict its collections to objects having local historical significance. This solution will demonstrate the integrity of the museum's motives and will win the respect and good will of the leaders of the community. It may antagonize some potential donors, but it is more likely to win the support of others to whom the purposes of the institution have been clarified by the refusal to accept offered gifts.

The adoption of such a clear-cut decision may seem to be an impossible reversal of policy in small museums already possessing miscellaneous collections. The change of course cannot be accomplished immediately. But the policy could be adopted as an objective to be achieved over a five- or ten-year period. It would require the gradual elimination of materials not relevant to the scope of the collections, by returning them to their former owners, by placing them in other museums as exchanges or gifts, or by offering them for sale through appropriate commercial outlets.

The small history museum which is primarily concerned with the story of the community in which it is located is most likely to succeed as a public service institution if it restricts the scope of its collections to objects having local historical significance. The quality of these collections will be determined by the relative historical value of the individual articles in them.

HISTORICALLY SIGNIFICANT OBJECTS

The question immediately arises as to how the relative historical value of an individual article can be established. It seems reasonable to assume that its historical worth is determined by the contribution it makes to the knowledge of history. Considerable confusion has resulted from the failure to apply this criterion critically. There is a widespread false assumption that all souvenirs, antiques, relics, and heirlooms must by definition have historical significance. There is a mistaken tendency to assign historical importance to the sentimental, romantic, nostalgic, and aesthetic connotations of individual objects. The age and apparent associations of an object cannot be used as the only criteria for establishing historical value. A fist-sized pebble, taken from the fields of Gettysburg and placed in a museum case, is certainly old and was definitely associated with the site of a great historic event. However, it is clearly incapable of throwing any light upon the battle it witnessed. A few less extreme examples may aid in clarifying this misconception of the meaning of the term "historical value.".

An old letter attached to a handkerchief with an embroidered design in one corner states that it was given to the great-grandmother of a local citizen by a famous political figure when he visited the community in the 1850's. This is a romantic souvenir of an insignificant historic incident. It has historical value only as an example of the type of embroidery done in the 1850's

An old chair purchased a few years ago from a dealer in antiques does not have any written record of its individual history. By comparison with published photographs and descriptions of similar chairs possessing authoritative records, it is found to be a Hitchcock chair made in the early nineteenth century in New England. This antique has historical value as an undocumented example of a type of furniture in common use in the eastern United States between 1820 and 1840.

An affidavit certifies that a six-inch piece of rope is a fragment of the one used to hang a notorious criminal in the 1880's. This relic may be morbidly interesting as a curiosity, but it contributes no information about the historic incident with which it is associated. It merely demonstrates that ropes used in the 1880's are identical to those that may be purchased today in a hardware store. This relic has no historical significance.

An American flag with forty-four stars was crocheted about 1894 by the grandmother of a civic leader. This heirloom may have sentimental value for some of the descendants of the maker. It is a unique, atypical item. Normally flags are not crocheted. Its proportions and the colors of the yarns used do not meet standard specifications. It is not a characteristic product of the early 1890's. It has no historical value.

An historically significant object contributes to a clearer understanding or interpretation of some former custom, activity, episode, or personality. The extent of this contribution depends upon 1) its documented individual history; 2) its physical character and condition; 3) the nature of the historic period or episode with which it is associated.

A complete documentary record of an object should include a description of the circumstances under which it was found or made and by whom, a report of how and by whom it was first used, and a chronological outline of its subsequent history. Contemporary records and other papers may contain internal evidence of the truthfulness of the statements made in them. On the other hand, the information given may be based upon family tradition and upon hearsay, the details of which cannot be verified. The record may contain statements made in good faith that are demonstrably inaccurate historically. It is necessary to evaluate critically the contents of the written records accompanying an historic article. Authentic documentation gives an object an historical individuality that can be acquired in no other way.

The physical character of the object should enable an observer to visualize more clearly some custom or activity of the past. The more commonplace and ordinary an article once was, the more likely it is to reflect accurately the social environment in which it was used. Certain articles that have always been rare, either because of inspired craftsmanship or because of the materials of which they were made, are highly prized for their aesthetic qualities as well as for their historical significance. Yet many of them are likely to be less valuable historically than the more widespread and casual articles which were contemporary with them. Unique objects, resulting either from accident or from the whim of their makers, have little historical value. Because there is no other article like any one of them, they cannot, as a class, illustrate or clarify former customs or activities, regardless of the authenticity or detail of the record which accompanies them.

Many objects may have historical value because of their physical character even when unaccompanied by documented individual histories. Among them are examples of styles of furniture, costumes and uniforms, types of chinaware and glass, and characteristic forms of household utensils and farm and industrial implements. Individual items in these several categories may be assigned accurately to specific historic periods, and even limited geographical areas, by comparing their physical characteristics with published photographs and descriptions of similar objects which are known to have authentic individual histories. Through such accurate identifications these undocumented articles achieve value as examples of recognized classes of historical materials.

The historical value of an article is directly proportional to its physical condition. A complete object in the approximate condition it was in when in normal use clearly reflects the social environment of which it was a part. Its original finish, the patina of age, and minor alterations caused by normal and continuous use enhance its charm and historical value. An attempt to restore such an object to its condition when new tends to destroy some of its usefulness as an historical item.

Broken and incomplete objects, and those badly mutilated because of neglect or exposure, have lost most of their historical value. Their dilapidated condition prevents their use as an aid in the interpretation of the customs or activities with which they were once associated. In some cases objects may be restored approximately to their original condition by making careful repairs. In other instances, a complete composite article may be constructed by using parts of several incomplete but essentially identical items. Such restorations of museum pieces are permissible, provided accurate and detailed records of the repairs and substitutions are kept among the documents relating to each object. These restored and repaired articles may be useful for illustrative purposes, but they are clearly not authentic historic pieces, and must be so designated when placed on display.

When a portion of an historic object is so fragmentary or mutilated that it can be identified only by reference to the documents which accompany it, it has become a relic, which, by definition, is "some remaining portion or fragment of that which has vanished or is destroyed." Examples of relics are: a piece of wood from a naval vessel that saw action in the War of 1812; a badly rusted section of a bayonet blade picked up on a Civil War battlefield; a lock of hair from the head of a famous person; a piece of stone or plaster taken from an historic building. All of these and similar relics may have some interest as curiosities, but most definitely do not have any historical value.

The third criterion by which the relative significance of an historic object may be judged is the nature of the historic period or episode with which it is associated. For example, there are two similar desks which were used contemporaneously for approximately the same number of years. The first served as the desk of the mayor in the city hall. The second, possibly a better and more typical piece of furniture, was used by an obscure but respected

merchant in the community. It is probable that the first will be
considered the more significant historically, because of its association with a number of important events in the history of the
community's government. Or again, there are two identical flags.
One was carried during the Civil War by the regiment recruited
from among the citizens of the community. The other was flown
for a number of years from the flag pole in front of the armory.
Both have historical value, but greater significance will be assigned to the flag that participated in the historic battles of the
Civil War. The principal of status through association is certainly
valid in the field of historical objects. The historical significance
of an object will be enhanced if it can be shown to have been
associated in some manner with important and well-known periods, events, or individuals in history.

The variability inherent in these three criteria—documentation, physical character, and historical association—and the di-
versity of opinion concerning the interpretation of each of these,
prevents the formulation of categorical and detailed rules for determining the historical significance of an object. In the last
analysis the usefulness of an object as a means of understanding
and interpreting history must be decided by the officials of the
museum in whose collections the object is located, through the
dispassionate application of these three criteria and in accordance
with the interests and objectives of the institution.

The collections of history museums may be grouped into four
general categories. The first of these contains objects that possess
historical individuality because of the authentic documentary
records relating to each of them, their physical characteristics and
good condition, and their association with well-known historic
periods, events, or individuals. These are the articles that possess
the most significance historically. However, it is probable that as
a group they comprise only a relatively small portion of the total
collections.

The second category, which is probably the most numerous,
consists of authentic historical pieces that have doubtful or incomplete individual records, or no records at all. Their historical
value is achieved by their identification through comparison with
known, authentically documented articles, either directly or by
means of published photographs and descriptions. Because of
these accurate identifications they do make useful and legitimate

contributions to a clearer understanding or interpretation of former customs, activities, and episodes.

The third category comprises a group of articles that are useful in interpreting history, but have no inherent historical value. They are modern replicas, either full-size or miniature, of known authentic historic pieces. Many museums use such objects, properly designated as reproductions, to fill important gaps in their collections, to complete displays of closely associated objects as in period rooms, and to illustrate in exhibits the larger historical materials, such as the various means of transportation and significant buildings, which could not otherwise be shown. The most elaborate use of miniature replicas is found in dioramas.

Under the fourth category are grouped various miscellaneous articles, mostly relics, which have been saved because they are old, or are strange and unusual, or have doubtful associations that invite sentimental or romantic responses. If these articles are judged on the basis of their usefulness in interpreting history, the vast majority of them will be found to have no historical significance and should be discarded as worthless.

WAYS AND MEANS OF ACQUISITION

When the scope and quality of the collections have been determined, it becomes necessary to work out procedures to be followed in the course of their expansion. In the case of collections limited to articles having a demonstrable relationship to local history, the decision as to whether an object should be accepted by the museum depends first upon whether it has the necessary associations, and second upon whether it will be useful. A valid conclusion requires a knowledge of the community's history and a familiarity with the materials already in the museum's possession.

Many small history museums fail to pay sufficient attention to these two considerations. Frequently the individual temporarily in charge will accept an article if it looks old, without evaluating it, partly because of a readily acknowledged feeling of incompetence to give a critical opinion, and partly because it seems better to keep an irrelevant or useless item than to lose something which later may prove to have considerable historic significance.

If a small museum is unable to employ a trained staff member capable of making these critical decisions, it would be sensible to insist that the article be accepted provisionally by the person on duty. Final acceptance or rejection should be made by the museum board or a responsible committee possessing the information required for reaching a sound decision. This is one of the arguments justifying the creation of an accession committee of the board. Its members, it may be added, must have the qualifications to pass judgment or should get the advice of qualified persons.

An inevitable result of the possession of the knowledge required to judge critically whether or not an item should be added to the collections is the realization that the museum collections are incomplete and that their contents do not cover their intended scope adequately. Certain episodes, customs, and periods in the community's history may be illustrated profusely, while others of equal or greater importance may have sparse or no representation. The passive attitude of accepting gratefully appropriate additions to the collections as and when they are offered will, in most instances, increase the number of articles illustrating periods and customs already well represented and, at the same time, will make more conspicuous the gaps created by the absence of articles with other associations.

Obviously it is in the best interests of the museum for the board or its accession committee to use the knowledge required for the critical evaluation of possible accessions as the basis for formulating a positive and long-term program of collection expansion. An outline of the community's history correlated with the museum's holdings will dramatize the nature and extent of the existing gaps. A list of desired articles in order of priority of need could be widely publicized among the museum membership and with the cooperation of various civic and cultural organizations. After all, the entire community will benefit if the museum possesses well-rounded and reasonably complete collections of materials which will enable it to interpret fairly and completely the story of the community's development.

There are several ways in which a museum acquires additions to its collections. The most frequent one is through gifts or donations. Less often, materials may be obtained as the result of purchases, exchanges, or loans.

Gifts are received in a variety of ways. They may result from extended and formal negotiations, or from a neighborly and casual incident. They may be the product of more or less adroit suggestions from a museum official. In any event it is vitally necessary to make sure that an immediate record is made of the circumstances accompanying their receipt. Otherwise misunderstandings may arise.

Some individuals are reluctant to lose all contact with the material given the museum, and attempt to make the gift contingent upon the fulfilment of certain stipulations. Among the more common of these are the requirements that the gift always be on display; that the name of the donor or some designated relative be included prominently in the display; and that all the items in the gift be kept together physically, both in the files and on display. On the other hand, the museum cannot afford to make any agreement that will restrict the reasonable use of its own property. The gift agreement must indicate clearly that the legal title to the articles in question is transferred without conditions or reservations by the donor to the museum. It is generally agreed in the museum world that gifts which are qualified by any conditions whatever should be declined as gracefully as possible.

Most small museums do not purchase additions to the collections because funds are not available for such a purpose. If, however, some fortunate museum can buy materials, a careful check should be made on the authenticity of each article and its relative market value, prior to its purchase. Sometimes a disinterested and competent appraiser in the community will give his assistance, or advice and expert opinion may be requested from some nearby larger museum. Lack of funds does not mean that the museum is completely unable to obtain articles that are for sale. The situation may be called to the attention of an appropriate friend of the museum, with the suggestion that if he makes it possible for the museum to possess the materials, they will be recorded in the museum's books as a gift from him, with the accompanying newspaper releases if desired. The value of such gifts is deductible for income tax purposes, under certain conditions.

Exchanging articles with other museums is a method of increasing collections which is slowly gaining popularity among history museums. It is common practice in natural history museums. There are two reasons for encouraging exchanges of collection items between history museums: first, it is proper that significant historical materials be located in the area with which they are associated, and if some have strayed they should be returned to the local museum in that area which is equipped to care for them; second, duplicate and surplus materials that belong in a clearly defined class of historic objects, but lack specific local associations in one museum, may be used to fill gaps in the collections of another. Of course the complete record of the exchange should exist in the correspondence and related documents.

Newly organized small museums are inclined to accept gratefully interesting materials as indefinite loans from local citizens in order to improve the appearance of their recently arranged exhibit cases. Quite a number of small history museums have in their collections articles accepted at various times in the past as long-term loans. This means that these museums are responsible for property that does not belong to them. This is bad business practice. The leaders among museums urge strongly that small museums scrupulously avoid this practice as a means of enhancing a museum's collections.

The motives of both parties are suspect. The museum, the borrower, seeks to impress its visitors by displaying objects which it does not own, an apparently harmless subterfuge which is nevertheless contrary to museum ethics and integrity. The lender may, quite altruistically, feel that the loan will help in the museum's development. However, the lender's failure to present the objects as a gift implies a lack of faith in the museum's future. There may be other motives involved. The lender, no longer able to care for the materials conveniently, may lend them for an indefinite period to the museum in order to avoid paying the charges asked by a commercial storage warehouse. Or again, social prestige and self-importance may be inflated by reference publicly to the attractive personal property on loan to the museum. Lenders can become administrative nuisances. They or their heirs may object to the ways in which their loans are used and cared for. A sensible procedure is to take immediate steps to transform any existing long-term loans into gifts, or to arrange their return to their owners or their heirs.

There is one exception to the general rule not to accept loans. This is the short-term borrowing by the museum officials of one or more items from private or corporate owners, or from other museums, for the purpose of using them to fill gaps in a special exhibit.

This is frequently done in art museums. The objects are borrowed for a few weeks, or a month or two. They are brought to the museum just before they are put on display, and are returned to the lenders immediately after the exhibit is dismantled. Of course the entire transaction must be recorded on appropriate forms.

Regardless of whether the addition to the collections is a gift, a purchase, an exchange, or a temporary loan, it constitutes a business transaction. As a transfer of ownership in the first three forms and a transfer of custody in the case of the short-term loan, the transaction should be recorded in a formal and preferably legally valid document of agreement.

Such documents may take many forms. The essential elements are, however, that two identical copies of the record of the transaction be made and signed by both parties, each of whom retains one copy. The form may be an elaborate document resembling a citation or diploma, with the name of the previous owner of the material in large letters, or it may be simply a formal letter from a museum official to the former owner, a copy of which is countersigned and returned to the museum. It is customary to include in the citation or the letter the conditions under which the museum accepts the materials, the nature of the release agreed to by the former owner, and a brief listing of the objects involved. Occasionally, the record of transfer is drawn up as a legal document, prepared and approved by lawyers representing both parties to the transaction.

The addition to the collections, whether it be a single item or a group of many items, which is acquired by the museum in the transaction involving the transfer of ownership, is generally designated an "accession." The documents relating to this transaction are known collectively as the "accession record."

Once the museum officials have accepted an accession, the complex processes of documentation and preservation begin.

DOCUMENTATION

The historical significance of an object lies not in itself alone but also in the information relating to it. Everything that is known about it, whether fact, tradition, or hearsay, should be recorded in permanent form. The object and its written record must be so clearly connected that there can be no possible doubt concerning its identity. This is the reason why systematic collection records must be maintained in every museum.

It is, of course, impossible to prepare a complete identifying document for each object and to insure that it will be physically attached to the object permanently. Museums long ago began using identification symbols. A single number in a series, attached to both the object itself and to its written record, will provide a permanent identity of the physical object with information relating to it. The degree of absolute identification is only as good as the infallibility of the numbering system adopted and the way in which it is used.

The assignment of this identifying number to an object constitutes registering it in the museum's collections. This process is often referred to erroneously as "cataloging," a faulty usage which is apt to cause confusion between two distinct procedures.

To register an object is to assign to it an individual place in a list or register of the materials in the collections in such a manner that it cannot be confused with any other object listed. Its individuality is established by linking its place in the list with the information that accompanied it when it was received by the museum. This is done by applying the same number to both the object and its written record. Thereby the identifying number becomes the registration number. No additional information is needed to maintain the permanent and absolute individuality of the object.

To catalog an object is to assign it to one or more categories of an organized classification system so that it and its record may be associated with other objects similar or related to it. In order to insure accuracy in making this assignment time and expert knowledge are required. The object needs to be studied with care, identified explicitly, and compared skillfully with other similar objects. However, the cataloging or classifying of an object can in no way alter or invalidate the significance and function of its registration number.

The failure to distinguish clearly between registering and cataloging has led either to an assumption that objects must be classified before they can be registered, or to an attempt to establish a registration system that will also serve as a means of classifying materials. In either instance, the registration process is retarded and the attempted fusion of the two distinct procedures causes complications and confusion. The registration number, altered in an effort to have it indicate catalog categories as well, tends to become so intricate that it loses some of its value as a means of identification and yet fails to function satisfactorily as a catalog number.

The oldest and apparently simplest registration system is to assign numbers in a single series to the articles in the order in which they are accepted by the museum. That is, item 1318 is the one received next after item 1317, regardless of the source or nature of the materials or the time which has elapsed between their arrivals. The essential element of this system and of several variants derived from it is the consecutive numbering of the objects in the order of their receipt. This creates a serious practical problem. If an accession contains only one item, its registration number can be assigned without delay and the process can be applied immediately to the next accession. However, when an accession consists of an indefinite and large number of articles, considerable time must be devoted to registering each of these before the numbers for the items in the next accession can be determined. Inevitably the assignment of registration numbers to individual articles progresses more slowly than the rate of receipt of accessions. The constantly expanding lapse of time between the receipt of an object and its registration increases the danger of losing vital information that should be in the record, and may even result in incorrect identification.

A widely used and practical numbering system that overcomes this difficulty is one recommended by the American Association of Museums in its publication *Museum Registration Methods*. Under this system, the accessions of each calendar year are numbered consecutively in the order of their receipt. To distinguish one annual series from another, the last two digits of the current calendar year with a decimal point precede the accession number. Let us assume accession 58.27 is the last one received in the year 1958. The next accession, the first received in 1959, then carries the number 59.1.

The accession number cannot serve as the registration number. The accession number identifies with a single number all of the materials, be they few or many, contained in the accession. However, this is easily remedied by giving each article a place in a closed serial number series limited to materials in the accession.

By adding this object number with a decimal point to the accession number, a three-part registration number is achieved that clearly identifies the individual object. By way of illustration, the registration number 58.17.12 is the symbol for the twelfth article in the seventeenth accession received by the museum during the year 1958. Let us assume that the next accession received contains fifteen articles which are numbered serially from 1 to 15 inclusive. Their registration numbers would be 58.18.1 through 58.18.15.

An object composed of several elements, each of which is a complete entity but also an essential part of the larger complex, such as a cup and saucer, or a complete military uniform, should be given a single registration number. If it seems advisable to distinguish between the several discrete elements of the object, each may be identified by adding a different lower case letter to the object unit of the number. Thus, if 58.17.12 is a cup and saucer, the cup would carry the number 58.17.12a, and the saucer 58.17.12b.

When this three-part registration number is observed upon a specimen, it immediately indicates approximately how long the item has been in the collections by the first unit, the year number; it furnishes the means of determining the source of the object and the materials with which it is associated by the second unit, the accession number; and it establishes the individual identity of the item by the third unit, the object number.

The most practical value of this three-part registration system is the elimination of the principal cause for the accumulation of an expanding backlog of recently received materials not yet registered. Because the individual object number is part of a closed series restricted to a single accession, the registration of the contents of each accession is an independent operation unaffected by the current status of the registration process in any other accession. For example, the five articles in the accession received this morning can immediately be given their permanent registration numbers, in spite of the fact that the fifty or more articles comprising the accession acquired yesterday have not yet all been registered.

It has already been stated that some form of informal written record should be made immediately upon receipt of an accession, including the assignment of the accession number. To prevent accidental duplication a notebook should be kept close at hand in which the essential facts of each accession may be entered, line by line, as follows:

    58.13—March 6—Mary Jones—six cups and saucers

    58.14—March 10—Henry Smith—Mayor Smith's watch chain

    58.15—April 2—Jim Duggan—his father's surgical instruments.

The permanent accession record, based upon the informal notes taken at the time of arrival, should be prepared as soon as practical. The single line notations then may be crossed out individually, as evidence that the permanent record has been completed.

The record of the accession may be prepared in permanent form before the registration of its contents is completed. When the numerical list of the items in each accession has been incorporated into its permanent record, the file of accession records becomes the museum register, the most important single document in the museum. Within its pages lies the key to the individual identity of each object in the museum's collections. The responsibility for its maintenance and care should be assigned to a single person, either the ranking member of the museum staff, or a responsible member of the museum committee of the governing board, if the museum cannot yet afford a full-time staff.

The physical form of the museum register may be adapted to the desires of those who work with it, provided its function and security are not compromised. A convenient and attractive arrangement is to use standard letter-size paper. Each accession record is entered upon a separate sheet. These are then filed serially by accession number in a notebook, and permanently bound at the end of each calendar year when the registration for that period has been completed.

The sheet on which the permanent accession record is typed should be a printed or mimeographed form, consisting of a series of headings or captions so distributed over the page as to allow space for entering the necessary information under each. The use of a form prevents the unintentional omission of necessary information and insures that analogous data appear in the same relative position on each record. It is customary to reserve about a third of the page for listing the objects in the accession. If the accession contains a large number of objects, this list may be continued upon the back of the form and on supplementary sheets, each marked with the identifying accession number. The permanent record should be typed in duplicate, in order that the original may be filed immediately for safe keeping and the carbon may become available as a work sheet until the registration of the contents is completed. The notes taken as a temporary record at the time of the receipt of the accession may be recorded in longhand on copies of the accession form, subject to later revision and transcription.

The essential information needed in each accession record includes the following items:

1. *Accession number*: This two-unit number should appear in the upper right-hand corner of the form.

2. *Source*: The name and address of the previous owner, the individual or organization from whom the material has been received, as well as the manner of its receipt, whether by purchase, bequest, gift, or exchange.

3. *Date of receipt*: The date or dates on which the accession was received and accepted as an addition to the collections.

4. *Description*: A brief statement of the nature of the accession, followed by a list containing a short description of each article, preceded by its object number, that is, the third unit of its registration number.

5. *Origin*: When and where the objects were made or found and, if possible and appropriate, by whom and how used.

6. *Remarks*: All available information about the accession.

These headings, and any useful additional ones, may be arranged on the form as desired. The notes under each heading may be brief or elaborate, according to the policies of the individual museum and the circumstances associated with the several accessions.

The second indispensable step in the registration process is to mark each item in each accession with its three-part registration number, in such a manner that this symbol will permanently link the object with its record in the museum register. This is done by either painting or sewing the number onto the article.

On firm surfaces artists' oil paints are used. The most satisfactory color is Chinese vermilion because it can be seen easily against almost any background color. The paint is mixed with quick drying oil on a small palette until it has the consistency of ink. The number is then written upon the object with a fine brush or a crow-quill pen. When the paint is dry it should be covered with a transparent coating of plastic, celluloid, or shellac, to insure its permanence. If the surface is too porous to receive the paint satisfactorily, repeated applications of a solution of celluloid-acetate to a small area will fill the pores with celluloid, creating a smooth surface upon which the number may be painted.

The registration number cannot be painted on clothing, textiles, and some types of baskets. These may be identified by placing the number on a cloth laundry-marking tag and sewing it on, or attaching it with rust-proof staples such as are used in laundries. Under no circumstances use either pins or ordinary staples to attach these cloth numbers to textiles. They will surely leave rust marks.

The number should be placed on some inconspicuous spot, such as the base, the back, or the interior of the object, so that it will not be visible when the article is used in exhibits. The size of the number painted or sewn on the article will, of course, depend somewhat upon the size of the article. As long as the digits are legible and seen easily, they need not be conspicuous. With a little practice, very small but still legible numbers can be achieved.

Several methods of marking objects, which unfortunately are sometimes used, should be avoided. The practice of attaching a cloth or paper tag to the object by means of a string or wire is dangerous. The string or the tag may be easily broken or torn. It is inadvisable to use paper labels, glued, sewed or tacked to the object, as a time-saving expedient. The paper becomes brown and brittle with age, and is easily torn. The numbers on the paper may fade, and become smudged or illegible. Gummed labels will dry out, curl up, and fall away from the object. Writing the number directly on the article with a pen or a crayon should be avoided for it may be partially or completely rubbed off accidentally.

There are three supplementary record files associated with or derived from the museum register which have proved useful in small museums. They are the document file, the donor file, and the object file.

The majority of accessions to the museum collections acquire at one time or another various documents which should be associated with them. These include correspondence, legal documents, lists, inventories, and notations made by the former owners, records of temporary loans, photographs, newspaper releases, and various research data. Papers of this nature relating to a single accession should be kept together in a document file. This consists of manila folders or envelopes housed in a standard letter or legal size filing cabinet. The folders, each labelled with its identifying number, are arranged serially by accession numbers. In this way all documents relating to an accession are kept together and are easily accessible. The second copy of the accession form in the museum register can be placed in this file when the registration process has been completed.

It is important for museum officials to maintain good relations with those who have contributed to the collections of the museum. It is advisable, therefore, to establish the donor file, which provides an easy and rapid means of ascertaining the nature and number of accessions received from a single source, whether that be an individual, an organization, or a commercial firm. The name and address of each source is entered on a standard file card which is then placed alphabetically in the donor file. On each card, under the name of the source, are listed the numbers of all accessions received from that source, often accompanied by a brief descriptive phrase. Additional information may be obtained without delay by turning to the indicated accession form in the museum register.

When occasion arises to determine the quantity and variety of a class of objects in the collections, such as Indian pottery, guns, or household utensils, it becomes necessary to search the museum register, accession record by accession record, to locate the items sought. This tedious chore can be avoided by establishing an object file in which each card carries the record of a single object in the collections, including its registration number, a brief description, its location in the museum, and such other information about it as seems desirable. If these cards are arranged serially by accession numbers, then the object file becomes merely an unnecessary duplication of the museum register. However, if the cards are arranged by categories, such as clothing, furniture, ceramics, weapons, farm implements, and other subjects, the object file becomes a useful supplement to the museum register. The number and variety of categories used in the file will depend upon the interests and needs of those working with the collections.

This object file is the museum catalog. It may be developed gradually as need arises by making cards for the individual objects located each time the museum register is searched for a class of material. Or it may result from the routine task of making individual cards for each of the objects in an accession immediately upon the completion of the registration process.

In museums with collections of only a few thousand objects there is a tendency to put similar things together. Ceramic pieces are placed on one set of shelves; clothing is assembled in a restricted group of cabinets; furniture is accumulated in some special area. This segregation of materials establishes, in effect, a physical catalog of the collections.

The preparation of an object file, or museum catalog, involves considerable time and energy, and keeping it currently abreast of the accessions as they are received is a never-ending obligation. In a small museum this file may be a valuable accessory to, but is not an indispensable part of, the museum's documentary record. The officials of each small museum should determine independently whether or not the usefulness of a museum catalog is sufficiently great to justify the amount of work required to prepare and maintain it.

Before leaving the subject of collection documentation, some consideration must be given to the matter of correlating the records of materials that have been in the collections for a number of years with this recommended registration system. Questions that may arise can be resolved most readily by keeping constantly in mind that the primary purpose of collection documentation is to insure the permanent and individual absolute identification of each item in the collections.

If the records of the older collections do preserve adequately the individual identity of the objects they contain, then there is no need to change the older registration system merely for the sake of conformity. There is little likelihood that the older identification numbers will be confused with the suggested three-part registration numbers. In many instances, however, the older documentation may be confused and incomplete. Several successive attempts to establish practical numbering systems may have resulted in an apparent duplication of numbers. Vital information on accessions may be missing, such as dates of receipt, names of former owners, or lists of accession contents.

Individual identification of objects in the older collections, in terms of the known but incomplete information on each, can be achieved by adapting the existing records to the three-part registration system through the use of arbitrary symbols, and to the new accession forms on which all available information is recorded, thereby explaining the use of the arbitrary symbols. When the year of receipt is unknown, a capital letter may be chosen as the symbol for a group of years. For example, the letter "c" might be applied to materials that are believed to have been received during the depression years and up to World War II, roughly 1934 and 1941. Similarly, accession numbers may be assigned arbitrarily when the date of receipt or the name of the source, or both, are unknown.

Illustrative examples of accession numbers may clarify this procedure:

C.1. All items probably received between 1934 and the beginning of World War II, for which neither the date of receipt nor the source are known, would be assigned this accession number. It might include several hundred object numbers.

C.2. During this same period Mr. Henry Black gave the museum, on various undated occasions, a variety of objects, all of which may be listed under a single accession number.

C.3. On one occasion, date unknown, Mr. Black contributed fifteen objects that can be definitely identified. These are given a separate accession number.

37.4. The records show that on October 3, 1937, Mr. Black gave the museum three still identifiable pieces of clothing, which constitute a single accession.

C.5. A number of articles in the collections are labelled, "Donated by Mrs. Mabel Brown." The dates of receipt are lost. Mrs. Brown became interested in the museum in 1934 and died in 1942. All of these articles may appropriately be listed under a single accession number.

Let us assume that a small museum has decided to adopt the recommended three-part registration system, effective at the beginning of the current calendar year. It finds that the records of the collections it already possesses are so confused and fragmentary that it is impossible to establish groups of materials which can be given arbitrary accession numbers. When it has been decided which of these materials are worth keeping, those to be retained should be numbered serially in the order in which they come to the hands of the person assigned the duty of marking them permanently. Since these serial numbers are restricted to those items received prior to the adoption of the new registration system, the process of numbering them becomes an operation independent of the current registration process, and therefore cannot retard or interfere with it. The register for those older materials could be a ledger in which the identification numbers are listed serially, accompanied by a brief description of the object to which the number refers.

PRESERVATION AND CARE

The small history museum should devote as much thought and care to the preservation of the materials in its collections as it does to choosing them and recording their story. Adequate accommodations need to be provided for filing them in an orderly manner which will insure their safety and their easy accessibility.

In many small museums the preservation of collections is confused with the exhibit program, resulting in the use of glass cases for the visible storage of the collections. This practice constitutes a prodigal waste of floor space and an improper use of exhibit facilities. Since the size of the collections usually increases more rapidly than either the number of glass cases or the space in which to place them, the cases become overcrowded and the need for additional floor space becomes critical. The exhibit program is only one of several ways in which some of the materials in the museum's collections may be used. It is the primary and most complex mechanism available to the museum for interpreting its objectives and its collections to the community it serves. This will be discussed in more detail later. In a well-managed museum a very clear distinction is made between the care and use of the collections and the function and organization of the exhibits.

The collections are the core of the museum's life. All of its activities are related to or derived from them. Their proper maintenance should take precedence over all other museum work. This principle is essential to good museum management.

Frequently those objects in a museum's collections that are not "on exhibit" are said to be "in storage." Psychologically the use of this word is unfortunate. It implies that these articles are of no current use to the museum and therefore are packed away in sealed boxes and cartons piled one upon another in small crowded back rooms and closets, a practice which is not uncommon.

The books conveniently arranged upon the shelves of the study at home are not "in storage" simply because they are not lying on the living room table immediately available for casual examination. Nor are the pieces of china and glassware on the shelves of the kitchen and pantry cupboards "in storage" because they do not happen to be laid out for display and use in the dining room.

Good housekeeping in a museum, as in a home, implies that most of the materials in the collections are kept in one or more rooms, not open to the public, in an orderly fashion which will make them available on short notice to either staff members or students for examination, study, and use. These study and reference files are compactly arranged in tiers of shelves and in sets of drawers, multiplying the available filing space by many times the floor space in each room.

These collection filing rooms have certain attributes in common, regardless of their respective sizes or the materials they contain. The most efficient use is made of every available inch of shelf and drawer space in which objects may be placed. All objects are covered, either in drawers, in cartons and paper boxes, or in plastic or cloth dust covers. These various containers all have labels attached to them on which are listed the nature of the contents. And finally, most of the rooms will also contain a table upon which the contents of a box, carton, or drawer can be spread for examination.

Because it is a normal practice in good housekeeping, it is almost taken for granted in a museum that objects of similar use and materials will be placed together in these files. Thereby a rough sorting, a physical cataloging into major classes, is achieved. This aids in the location of any object sought for examination and study or for use in the exhibits.

The apparent crowded conditions in some small museums may lead to the assumption that collection files cannot be developed until better accommodations are secured. Such a delay is not necessary. It is more important to preserve the materials in the collections safely and efficiently than it is to maintain extensive but crowded and unattractive exhibits.

Space for collection files can be obtained by using one of several exhibit rooms for the purpose, or by erecting a temporary partition across one end of a large exhibit hall. A surprising number of objects can be kept in a properly equipped filing room. By transferring the less interesting and duplicate materials from the exhibits to the files, the apparent overcrowding of the museum vanishes. The establishment of collection files in rooms not open to the public results in more convenient facilities for working with and studying the collections. It also provides less crowded, better arranged exhibits, the attractiveness of which more than compensates for any necessary loss of display space.

The filing room can be equipped easily. Adjustable steel shelving and steel filing cabinets can be purchased if funds are available. However, any carpenter or reasonably competent amateur can build simple but adequate wooden shelving and tiers of drawers. Sometimes these may be obtained cheaply or as gifts from local merchants who in remodeling their stores have discarded this type of equipment. The various containers for the items in the collections can be secured by picking up at the local stores the needed cartons and paper boxes, which would otherwise be thrown out as trash. The arrangement should not be considered as a request for a personal favor, but rather as an opportunity for the stores to render a service to a public institution. Small plastic boxes and vials can be bought in variety and drug stores. When the most appropriate sizes of boxes have been determined through experience, orders can be placed for custom-made containers at a paper-box factory.

Articles placed in unmarked boxes and cartons are, for all practical purposes, lost until someone spends considerable time searching for them. It is extremely important that each container, large or small, be conspicuously marked with a list of its contents and their registration numbers. Some museum workers recommend placing a duplicate list inside each container. The time required to make a careful inventory of the contents of a box or carton before it is filed pays ample dividends in the time saved later in locating a desired object. When several smaller boxes containing similar materials are placed in a larger box the contents of each should be identified on an outside label.

If the filing room can accommodate a large table and has adequate ventilation, it can be used as a study room by visiting scholars, and as a demonstration room where objects from the collections may be laid out for, and handled by, school classes or adult study groups that have asked for such service, under the immediate supervision of a staff member.

Occasionally museum collections contain groups of materials that should not be discarded, but which, as far as can be determined, will not be used in any way in the foreseeable future. These may be placed in "dead storage," provided certain safeguards are met. Obviously materials that need periodic inspection to insure preservation should not receive such treatment. Objects in dead storage should be padded and braced to prevent breakage, and stored within reinforced wooden crates or boxes, ready for shipment anywhere by commercial carriers. Each container should be marked with a key number, or letter and number. A list of the contents needs to be prepared in triplicate. One copy should be placed inside the container, another attached, in an envelope if necessary, to the outside in a conspicuous position, and the third filed under an appropriate heading in the office files.

In addition to the provision of adequate facilities for the orderly filing and protection of the collections, individual attention should be given each object, for it must be preserved indefinitely. The first step is to make sure the article is clean. Surface dirt and stains must be removed, as well as any form of contamination that might affect other articles or the object itself.

As a matter of routine, wood, leather, textiles, and similar materials subject to insect damage should be fumigated when received. A closet or a specially constructed box that can be sealed tightly can serve as a fumigation chamber. It should be large enough to hold oversize textiles such as rugs and quilts and should be provided with an exhaust fan to clear the toxic fumes before the chamber is opened after use. If a museum cannot do its own fumigating, arrangements should be made with the local cleaners or a storage warehouse for the use of their facilities. Recent industrial advances have developed a variety of chemicals that may be used for fumigating. Some large museum or a pest control agency should be consulted concerning the most satisfactory fumigants to use for varying purposes and with the different classes of objects in the museum collections.

As a rule, common sense will determine the best method for cleaning an object. Some articles can be cleaned by dry brushing, others may be sponged or washed with mild soap and water. Great care should be taken to avoid changing the surface condition of an object, such as the color or texture of a painted surface or the discoloration of patina resulting from normal use. Most textiles can be cleaned commercially provided the pieces are not too fragile. Before sending textiles out to be cleaned, they should be inspected to establish that commercial cleaning will not shrink the fabrics or cause the colors in them to run or fade. In some museums those in charge prefer to wash more delicate and fragile clothing themselves.

When objects are received they may be broken or incomplete. The safest procedure in repairing museum items is the conservative one, for the principal objective is only to preserve the object. As a rule, repairs should be restricted to those which are necessary to prevent further deterioration. Some museum people consider it proper to restore an item to working condition, especially if it is to be used in exhibits. In any case it is common practice to indicate clearly, by color or material, the new portions replacing any missing or broken parts. When cleaning or repairing items in the collections remember the well-known museum admonition: "When in doubt—don't!"

Once the articles are cleaned, in good physical condition, and properly identified, they should be placed in the collection files with other similar objects. Thereafter their preservation depends upon the conditions under which they are filed. They must be protected against dust and dirt and extremes of temperature and humidity. Precautions must be taken to avoid fading through exposure to daylight and especially direct sunlight. Accidental breakage can be avoided by wrapping small fragile articles in cleansing or toilet tissues, or embedding them in a cushion of cotton batting in small containers. Larger fragile objects may be protected by custom built wooden or stiff wire frames and braces. Materials subject to destruction by insects should be filed in reasonably airtight cabinets or drawers containing some form of insecticide and inspected for possible damage at regular intervals of three months or so.

Professional museum technicians have devised a large number

of methods and recipes for use in the preservation of museum materials. The listing of these would require many pages. A few of the more generally recognized and wide-spread practices are given here.

No attempt should be made to clean oil paintings of any kind without the advice of an expert. The larger art museums can supply the names of qualified restorers of paintings. Although an expensive process, it is worthwhile.

Do not file costumes on ordinary wire hangers. They leave rust marks. If hangers are used, they should be padded and wrapped or made of wood or plastic. It is not wise to hang heavy costumes by the shoulders unless reinforced by a tape harness attached to the waistline. Otherwise they will sag, the seams will open, and the fabric may tear. In so far as possible, all textiles should be filed flat; if folded, a roll of tissue paper should be inserted in the folds to prevent creasing and breakage of threads, especially in silk.

Newspapers and printed or written documents of various sizes and types are frequently included in the collections of small history museums. Whether they consist individually of one or several sheets of paper, they should always be kept flat and unfolded in the files, preferably in cabinets consisting of large shallow drawers or in regular manuscript file boxes. Folded documents must be unfolded to be examined, and paper tends to become brittle, crack, and break along the folds. If a document is an appropriate part of an exhibit, a photostat or photograph of it should be used. Valuable documents should never be put on display. Light will discolor the paper and fade the ink. Photographic prints are subject to similar fading when left on display for extended periods.

The use of commercial cellophane tape should be scrupulously avoided in museum work. It contracts slightly with time, turns yellow, curls at the edges, and discolors and destroys the surface of any paper object to which it is attached. Documents may be repaired with another similarly packaged adhesive tape labelled "Permanent Mending Tape—for permanent paper mending." Printing and writing is legible through this tape.

The Interpretation

The small history museum is a public institution dedicated to the preservation and interpretation of historically significant objects. The responsibilities inherent in the performance of each of these two functions differ considerably. Yet they are, so to speak, the two faces of a single coin. Systematic and careful preservation of collections requires funds derived from the support given by the community and its interested citizens. This support is achieved by interpreting, through exhibits and related activities, the significance of the materials in the collections. Yet the interpretation, in turn, is dependent upon the systematic and careful preservation of the materials. Clearly the two functions are completely interdependent. Over-emphasis of one at the expense of the other defeats itself because the neglected function becomes so weakened it can no longer give the needed support to the dominant one.

In the larger well-equipped museum, blessed with adequate quarters and a diversified staff, the internal organization permits, at least in theory, the simultaneous performance of both museum functions. In small museums, seriously hampered in their aspirations by limited facilities and manpower, these two functions are usually given unequal consideration.

The officials of many small museums, convinced that public

support and good will are essential to the life of the institution, tend to concentrate upon the many activities connected with the interpretive function. As a result the organization, documentation, and management of the collections are so neglected that the materials in them cannot be identified easily or used effectively. Conversely, in other small museums interests are so largely confined to the accumulation and care of the collections that the function of interpretation suffers through neglect, and public good will and support, so essential to the proper performance of the function of preservation, are sacrificed.

The governing boards of small museums will need to recognize these dangers and establish procedures designed to avoid them. The factors influencing the decisions reached are largely individual in each museum—the size of the collections, the extent of documentation and of the filing facilities, the usefulness of the interpretive activities, and the needs and desires of the people of the community. It may be possible to establish a program of shifting emphasis, swinging at appropriate intervals from preservation to interpretation and then back again. Or it may be necessary to restrict the desirable activities in the performance of both functions, in order that comparable and simultaneous advance may be made in each. The development and growth of the institution may be less rapid, but certainly the progress made will be more stable, because it will be secured by equivalent expansion in each of the two interdependent museum functions.

Interpretation is achieved by using the materials in the collections, while preservation is concerned with assembling, documenting, and caring for them. The ways in which objects may be used to interpret history are almost endless. Through their critical comparison and study the knowledge of history may be expanded or clarified. Through their use in exhibits and other related museum activities they may render educational, informative, entertaining, and recreational services to people of all ages. The effectiveness of the methods used and of the results achieved is determined by the wisdom and insight employed in interpreting the significance of the historical source materials in the collections. Therefore the employment of all the activities and procedures connected with the use of these materials may properly be designated the function of interpretation.

The preceding pages have dealt with preservation. Those which follow have to do with interpretation.

STUDY AND INVESTIGATION

The historical significance of an item in the museum's collections depends upon the documented individual history connected with it, its physical character and condition, and the nature of the historic period or episode with which it is associated. The extent to which an object can be used in interpreting history depends in turn upon the completeness and accuracy of the museum records relating to it. The collections of even the smallest of local history museums contain objects that are potential source materials, through the study of which the knowledge of history, especially local and regional history, may be increased. Since every article may be subjected to more than normal scrutiny at some time, the compilation of authoritative records for each requires careful study and comparative investigations.

The primary source of information about an object is the individual or organization from whom it has been received, whether it be a gift, a purchase, or an exchange. The tendency is to record only the information essential for identification when the accession is accepted. Securing all available information on that occasion may seem to be an unnecessary chore and a waste of precious time. It is well to remember that the objects have been accepted because of their apparent historical significance, and not because they are additions to the collections. Comprehensive records should be made at the time the donor is prepared to give the information, or he may be asked to write out the information at his leisure and send it in to the museum.

Statements obtained from previous owners need to be verified and authenticated by consulting relatives and friends if feasible, by examining contemporary sources, such as newspapers, magazines, and photographs, and by comparing this information with that found in scholarly publications dealing with similar materials. Tradition and sentiment are inclined to affect the records associated with family heirlooms. It is disconcerting to discover in some reference book that an outmoded utensil said to have been a wedding present more than a hundred years ago actually was first manufactured fifteen years after the wedding date, or to find the name and 'address of a firm in a nearby town inconspicuously imprinted upon a wooden implement that the donor insisted had been hand-wrought by his grandfather. But it is most frustrating to encounter records that are incomplete because of the carelessness or ignorance of the recorder. In a midwestern museum a considerable number of objects of Indian origin, each apparently having noteworthy historical significance, are identified by "catalog" cards recording under both "source" and "origin" the single word "purchase." It is a heartbreaking experience for a scholar who appreciates the potential value of historic objects as source materials to find that the documentary records associated with them in many small museums are completely useless because they are either self-contradictory or incomplete.

Most small history museums cannot employ scholars to devote their full time to such investigations. However, this does not preclude such studies. The verification of the records is, of course, one of the staff responsibilities. Because of the pressure of other duties staff members usually do not devote sufficient time to it. They should be able to make a preliminary investigation and to enlist and guide the help of others. Perhaps the donor of the materials can be persuaded to establish the authenticity of his own statements. The museum may be able to secure the expert help of citizens with historical interests or of teachers in local high schools and colleges who are trained in historical work. The inquisitiveness of a museum volunteer may stimulate a critical study of the historical significance of some class of objects.

Small museums can encourage the interpretation of the materials in their collections through these and similar investigations by inviting students to study the collections and providing facilities to aid them in their work. Any citizen of the community, whether young or old, who can demonstrate his serious interest in history should be officially granted access to the filing room containing the materials with which he is concerned, and furnished, if possible, with a table and chair so that the materials being studied and the notes relating to them can be handled conveniently.

When these investigations result in manuscripts containing information of popular or general interest, the materials in the collections have indeed been interpreted in a manner that increases the knowledge of history. Such manuscripts should be published by the museum as informational leaflets or submitted in the name of the museum for publication in professional journals.

Research scholars in the field of history connected with other museums, with universities, or with research institutions at some distance from a small history museum may become interested in materials in its files. A scholar may wish to spend some time at the museum studying objects in its collections and the documentary records associated with them. If he is unable to journey to the museum he may ask to be furnished with photographs of objects and transcripts of the records relating to them. If the objects in which he is interested have critical significance as source materials for his studies he may request that they be loaned to him for a few weeks or months.

It is in the best interests of the small history museum to cooperate as fully as possible with out-of-town scholars, provided they are known to be responsible individuals associated with reputable institutions. The results of their studies may be added to the documentary records, thereby enhancing the historical significance of the objects concerned. These scholars customarily give appropriate credit in the published reports on their investigations to the museums, institutions, and individuals from whom they receive noteworthy assistance, including credit lines for illustrations, naming the organizations in which the objects shown may be found. This practice enhances the prestige of the small museum by bringing its name and its collections to the attention of other scholars and institutions.

An out-of-town scholar visiting a small history museum should be accorded every facility that will aid him in his studies, including permission to take such photographs as he desires. When the scholar asks by letter for assistance, every reasonable effort should be made to furnish the materials requested, including transcripts of records and photographs of objects. When furnishing photographs it is entirely proper for museum officials to stipulate that if they are published a credit line naming the museum must accompany them. Short-term loans of articles in the collections to scholars for study purposes should be permitted, provided the objects can be transferred to the borrower without danger of loss or destruction. This practice is a routine procedure in most natural history museums. The conditions governing a loan will normally be included in the correspondence, such as the items to be borrowed, the uses to which they will be put, how they will be cared for, and approximately when they will be returned. These conditions may be recorded more formally on a printed loan form to be signed by both the lender and the borrower.

Occasionally the assistance given out-of-town scholars leads to the discovery of clues that need to be explored through interviews, or followed into the records of other local organizations, such as newspaper or library files or government archives. When this is necessary, the museum can help by making arrangements to have some citizen, directly or indirectly connected with the museum, undertake the investigations the distant scholar needs to have made. As a rule most scholars will defray any reasonable expense incurred by the museum in rendering the various services requested.

There are many ways in which the small history museum without personnel trained in historical work and with inadequate facilities can make the objects in its collections available for use as source materials in advancing the knowledge of history. The authentication of statements in the documents associated with collection items, the encouragement of students desiring to study collection materials, and the assistance given out-of-town scholars are all a part of the function of interpretation.

EXHIBITS

In the nineteenth century visitors to a museum were admitted to exhibit halls where they could see the museum's treasures displayed in glass cases for protection against careless or acquisitive fingers. Traditionally the exhibits became identified with the museum as an institution, regardless of the other activities it performed. Since today, in the mid-twentieth century, most people still judge a museum by the character of its exhibits, these should reflect its policies and objectives. They are the show rooms in which the museum seeks to interest the visiting public in the services it has to offer.

History museums should not display articles just because they are antiques or curios. Exhibits are the most appropriate and dramatic means of demonstrating that historical objects are first-hand, tangible evidence of former customs, activities, and achievements. Their very existence helps to explain, illustrate, and enliven the community's past experiences. The successful transmission of this message emphasizes the importance of assembling and preserving these historically significant objects for the benefit of future generations as well as the citizens of today. In this way the exhibits justify the existence of the museum as a public service institution.

Each of the several historical subjects illustrated and explained by the exhibits is associated, directly or indirectly, with similar ones that preceded and followed it, thereby creating an historical continuity which becomes a visual expression of the community's composite memory. The ideal exhibit program of a history museum should demonstrate the living role that history can play in the life of the community by linking together the remembered yesterdays, the interesting todays, and the inevitable tomorrows. It is reported that Sir Winston Churchill once said, "The farther backward you can look, the farther forward you are likely to see." The exhibits of a museum constitute the most flexible and sensitive means it can use to fulfill the obligations inherent in its function of interpretation.

The exhibit program in each history museum differs from that in every other because it reflects the significant experiences of the community it serves and the attitudes and policies of the citizens who direct its destinies. This wholesome individuality prevents the formulation of detailed rules and instructions for creating historical exhibits. However, experimentation and experience have established some general principles and techniques of good museum display practices that are widely accepted in the museum world. These may be studied by those responsible for the exhibits in any small museum and adapted with initiative, ingenuity, and imagination to existing physical conditions and historical opportunities.

The principles to be followed in formulating a satisfactory exhibit program are derived from the concept that museum exhibits are created for the public. Their purpose is to interest, inform, and stimulate visitors and to encourage them to repeat an enjoyable and profitable experience. These principles are so

'general and fundamental that they can be adopted by any
museum, regardless of its size, the nature of its collections, the
extent of its exhibit space, or the scope of the facilities available
for constructing exhibits.

Museums, like other educational institutions, are entitled to
"academic freedom" of expression, but this privilege carries with
it a vital obligation. Exhibits must be objective and truthful, and
tell their stories without hint of bias or propaganda. Visitors
take it for granted that what they see and learn in museum
exhibits is accurate, trustworthy, and authentic. The dependabil-
ity of the information given is a measure of the institution's
integrity and, by inference, of that of the entire museum movement. Failure to meet these high standards amounts to the
forfeiture of a public trust. It does not pay to bluff or deceive
in arranging a display, either because of ignorance or for the sake
of expediency. Sooner or later a visitor will spot the subterfuge,
and embarrassment, at least, will result.

The objectives of an exhibit program can be achieved only by
retaining visitor interest. This is accomplished by leading the
visitor's attention from one object to another in an organized
display and from one display to the next in logical order. The
haphazard arrangement of displays, each containing miscellaneous objects, can result only in confusion and "mental indiges-
tion" on the part of the observer. The purpose of the exhibits
is lost in a welter of unrelated observations. A logical physical
arrangement of displays, each containing a well-arranged group
of related objects, is essential to a good exhibit program.

An axiom, derived from the fact that exhibits are still identified
with the museum as an institution, is: "Static museums are dead
museums." The installation of new exhibits and the rearrange-
ment of materials in existing ones have come to symbolize the
vitality of the institution. The changes need not be elaborate or
complex. It is sufficient merely to have some change, possibly
once a month, certainly once every three months. For example,
the furnishings in a period room could be adjusted to agree with
the seasons of the year. Short-term displays may feature recently
received collection items. Anniversaries, annual festivals such as
Thanksgiving and Christmas, and current community achievements invite the installation of temporary exhibits. Displays may
be revised and the objects in them rotated at intervals without

altering their themes. A successful exhibit program should include provision for the regular revision and improvement of existing displays and for the use of temporary exhibits.

In order that the message a display seeks to convey may reach the visitor, it is necessary to make him stop and look at it. This can be done by displaying prominently one or more objects which the observer associates immediately with some experience or information that is a part of his own fund of knowledge. This procedure is an adaptation of the well-known teaching device of "leading from the known to the unknown." The ability of visitors to identify themselves with subjects illustrated in the exhibits will kindle their interest and stimulate the desire for further examination.

Visitors to museum halls should be made to feel welcome. The popular homes in a neighborhood are those in which visitors feel welcome and at ease. This hospitable attribute is just as valuable to an institution as it is to a family. Visitors to museums should be greeted by an attendant when they enter and made to feel at ease by the interest taken in helping them to get acquainted with the exhibits. The atmosphere should be a friendly one, inviting the visitor to browse at his leisure from one display to the next, contemplating and then evaluating the enjoyment and the message he may derive from each. This hospitable and relaxing environment for the visitor must be planned and arranged, but its success depends upon its ready acceptance as a matter of course.

The application of these principles in a specific museum depends upon the actual, as well as the potential, role its exhibits may play in the life of the community. The reason for having public exhibit halls is to entice people to come and see the things that are on display and to become acquainted with the work of the museum. Good salesmanship requires the development of an attractive and convincing program that can challenge the competing interests in the community.

Many people think of a museum as a place to go only when they have nothing else to do, a way of spending leisure time. There are many leisure-time attractions in a community: lectures, concerts, movies, radio, television, organized sports—clearly the museum is in competition with other attractions, some of which are highly publicized and of professional quality. To challenge this competition a museum must offer a pleasant experience that is different, interesting, and stimulating. Potential visitors must be convinced that they want to see the exhibits rather than enjoy some other leisure-time experience.

First of all, the exhibit halls must be attractive and inviting. Just as a housewife devotes time and energy to decorating and furnishing the rooms of her home in good taste, so the museum officials should endeavor to establish a pleasing unity in the rooms containing the displays. The walls and ceilings should appear clean and fresh. The exhibit cases, which may be various types of equipment discarded by local merchants, can be transformed into modern, straight-lined units by masking ugly construction and distracting finishes with panels of plywood. Temporary and movable partitions, created by applying wallboard to two-by-four frames, will break the monotony of the case arrangements and supply additional display space. The walls and the cases should be painted in unobtrusive, quiet colors to furnish a suitable setting for the materials in the exhibits. The lighting fixtures should be modern and simple, yet give sufficient general illumination. Cleanliness in all details, including the contents of the displays, is of paramount importance. Even the condition of the air should be checked. It should neither have a musty, attic-dead odor nor should it advertise the nature of the janitor's supplies. If the ventilating facilities are inadequate to insure fresh, clean-smelling air, then sprays should be used regularly. The overall objective is to establish a tasteful and inviting environment for the exhibits. The visitor will approach the displays sympathetically, feeling that anything to be seen in such pleasant surroundings must be worth looking at.

Officials of many a small history museum may feel, sceptically, that these suggestions could apply to other museums but not to their own. The recognition of the need is the first major step to be taken. Altering the character of the exhibit rooms is neither difficult nor expensive. The use of initiative and energy is the principal requirement. A realistic estimate of the supplies and materials needed, and the practical application of imaginative planning and good taste, will achieve the desired results.

It is important that the exhibits have an easily recognized unity. A stranger visiting a museum for the first time will feel at ease and therefore interested if he can orient himself quickly.

Three different exhibit patterns may be followed in creating this desirable unity, depending upon the character of the materials in the collections and how the officials of a museum choose to interpret them.

One popular pattern found in many small history museums consists of showing similar examples of a single class of materials in each case. One showing ornamental glassware might be adjacent to one filled with porcelains. Across the aisle could be two other cases, one containing ladies' fans, the other ladies' shoes. Such displays can be attractive if they are not too crowded. They will be admired and examined by those interested in such materials. The great majority of visitors will recognize only that they emphasize the physical differences between essentially similar items.

Another exhibit pattern is that in which the exhibits demonstrate the developmental changes in a class of objects or in an activity. Each unit of such a pattern may occupy one or more display cases. For example, objects illustrating the story of lighting from the time of the torch and the candle, through the use of various types of oil lamps to the recent eras of illuminating gas and electricity, may well occupy three or four cases. Or the subject may be guns, from the flintlocks of the colonists to the modern hunting rifle. This exhibit pattern is widely used in history museums. It combines the concept of historical sequence with the desire to display similar things together. Its weakness lies in the forced isolation of the developmental story of a single class of materials torn from its historical context. It fails to show the contemporaneous changes that occurred in a variety of associated things and activities. Upon encountering this exhibit pattern, visitors will study the materials with which they are familiar and avoid those in which they are not interested.

The underlying concept of a third pattern differs from that used in the other two. Here the objects shown are subordinated to the interpretation of an historical theme rather than serving as the center of interest. Each unit of the pattern deals with some incident in history. Exhibit continuity is obtained by arranging these units in chronological order. The displays may be period rooms illustrating contemporary furnishings and related customs. Or they may be synoptic interpretations of significant historical events, such as the founding of the community, the establishment of the first public school, or the effects of some social or economic crisis. This exhibit pattern is the most difficult of the three to achieve, but it is the most satisfactory method of establishing unity in an exhibit program.

A museum must have a carefully organized and unified exhibit program in order to attract visitors and to challenge successfully the competing leisure-time attractions. Since exhibits constitute the most flexible and sensitive instrument the museum possesses for interpreting its collections and objectives, it should be self-evident that the continuity and living quality of history must be the theme that unites all elements of the exhibit program. All three exhibit patterns may be used, provided the one that interprets historical themes is dominant and the continuity of the story which unifies the entire program is not obscured. A well organized exhibit program will enable the visitor to orient himself quickly, to proceed through the exhibits in a logical manner observing and enjoying each successive display, and to depart with a better understanding of the meaning of history and convinced that the museum is an interesting and useful public institution.

The development of an organized exhibit program is a complex undertaking. Planning it on paper in detail, before starting its installation, is an efficient and time-saving procedure. The project may be treated as if it were a book with a series of chapter titles and subtitles. The outline of this imaginary book is then translated into the series of displays, each receiving attention in proportion to the importance of the subject that it interprets. As the exhibit plan unfolds, the available space for displays will require a reduction in the number of subjects dealt with in the outline and the abbreviation of the interpretation of each. This drastic editing of the project should recognize the anticipated attitudes and interests of the majority of expected visitors. When the continuity of the program has been achieved and the relative emphasis to be assigned each of its elements has been determined, the next step is to plan the organization of the individual displays, each of which should have internal unity. These details may be plotted on diagrams which can be compared easily and revised prior to installation. They should be scale drawings of the usable space in each case, on which the essential elements of the display may be drawn to scale.

There is always the danger of over-emphasizing the theme that a single unit of the program is intended to interpret. Its relation to the overall exhibit plan, as only one in a series of related displays, must be kept in mind constantly. The display in each case should be sufficiently attractive and interesting to win and hold the attention of the observer, and yet it should indicate clearly its relationship to the other displays. The continuity of the exhibit's message and the unity of the presentation is most apparent when the several individual displays elicit an equal degree of interest on the part of the observer.

As soon as work is begun upon the details of arrangement in individual cases, a new set of problems requiring decisions is encountered, such as the number and kinds of objects to be used and how they should be arranged; the nature of the accompanying charts, diagrams, or photographs; the size, number, and character of the textual explanations and interpretations; and the various colors and types of lighting appropriate to the theme of the display. The factors that must be considered in reaching these decisions differ so greatly among museums, because of their individuality, that detailed rules covering all situations cannot be given. It is possible to comment only upon a few practices which have come to be generally accepted.

Restraint needs to be practiced in using objects in the exhibits. There is of course the natural desire to show all of the articles of a kind in the collections. Yet a single and typical object, attractively displayed and carefully documented, will interpret a subject more clearly than a shelf full of similar articles differing only in details of interest to special students. Students should always have access to the materials in the collection files. A display contrasting examples of the plain and the ornamental modern frames for eye glasses when a pair of small-lensed steel spectacles, a lorgnette, and a pince-nez is bound to be more interesting than one showing eight or ten pairs of steel spectacles carefully laid out in a geometric pattern. Quantity of objects is no substitute for quality of display. A case crowded with objects, even if all are relevant to the subject illustrated, will repel rather than attract observers.

The use of historical objects alone will not create a satisfactory exhibit. They need to be accompanied by materials that assist in relating them to one another and in interpreting the subject in hand. In an historical display these accessory materials may be labels, photographs, maps, charts, diagrams, cut-out figures, or similar devices. The use of sound judgment and good taste in the choice and arrangement of these accessories is required to achieve appropriate balance between them and the objects they explain and interpret.

The labels, brief textual statements so essential in an exhibit that tells a story, are difficult to write. They should be brief, accurate, and unobtrusive. They should answer the questions aroused by the display and furnish sufficient information to stimulate interest in it. Labels may be classified according to their function: guide labels, master labels, subject labels, and object labels.

Single words or short phrases are used in the first two. The guide label may be attached conspicuously to the outside of the cases indicating the location of major divisions of the exhibits, such as "Indian Occupation" and "Pioneer Period." The master label refers to the subject of an exhibit unit, such as "Farms and Food," "Household Industries," and "Transportation." It is most frequently placed in the upper left corner of the display case and repeated in each of the cases housing the unit. Subject labels are more extended statements about elements within the unit. The object labels identify individual objects. Do not waste time labelling the obvious. A label beside an object, reading "silver spoon," is unnecessary. Labels may be printed, typewritten, hand-lettered, or built with plastic or cardboard letters. Be sure that the letters in the text are sufficiently large and legible to be read easily by people wearing bifocal glasses.

Subject labels are the most difficult ones to prepare. They must be as brief as possible. People generally will not read labels containing over seventy-five to one hundred words. The text should be restricted to stating the essential facts in a series of short sentences. Eliminate, in so far as possible, all adjectives, long words, and technical terms. An introductory complete sentence in the style of a newspaper headline will receive more attention than a one- or two-word title. This sentence should be emphasized by using letters which are larger or different in style and color from those in the body of the text. The message of the display should be grasped easily by reading the master label and the featured first sentences of the subject labels. If the text of a subject label must be lengthy, phrase it in several paragraphs, and treat each paragraph as a separate label.

Replicas and models may properly be included in exhibits, although they are not historically significant objects. Accurate full-scale reproductions of household furnishings, farm implements, mechanical devices, and similar objects may be included in displays when they are required to complete the continuity or the clarification of the subject being interpreted. It is essential, however, that the associated label clearly indicate that the object is a replica or reproduction. Miniature reproductions can serve the same purpose, provided they are accurate scale models. They are most useful as stand-ins for transportation equipment, buildings, and other complex constructions that are too large to be incorporated in the displays.

Dioramas depicting historical episodes in miniature are popular elements in a museum exhibit program. Highly realistic dioramas require expert craftsmanship and are correspondingly expensive. They may be obtained by contract from one of several artists in various parts of the country who specialize in making dioramas. The larger history museums should be able to supply names and addresses. Simple dioramas, actually three-dimensional pictures, may be constructed with plywood and cardboard as miniature stage settings under the direction of a competent artist. Forced perspectives should not be attempted in a diorama without complete knowledge of the technical considerations involved.

The unity so desirable in the entire exhibit program should also exist in the individual exhibit, whether it consists of one or several displays. Since it is in effect a three-dimensional picture it should possess the same attributes as a good painting. It must have good composition, balance, and appropriate emphasis in order to carry the observer's attention from one element to the next, leading to a complete appreciation of the subject it is designed to interpret.

Modern museums are using color to an increasing extent in their exhibits. The dead whites and greys, formerly so popular as background colors, are now being replaced by soft pastels. The lighter shades of blue and green are restful, while those of red and orange are stimulating. The background colors of individual cases may differ in order that each may be in harmony with the colors of the objects the display contains. The desirable unity may be obtained by using an appropriate color for the case exteriors and the walls of the room. Good taste and judgment must be exercised to avoid garish and displeasing color combinations. Brilliant, sharp colors should be avoided except when used for spectacular emphasis.

Proper lighting is an important factor in attractive exhibits. In many museums only artificial light is used in exhibit halls, but the absence of windows requires the use of some form of forced ventilation. In small history museums occupying former residences or rooms in public buildings, it may be impractical to block off the windows and install air conditioners. Natural illumination and ventilation must be used.

It is necessary to control natural lighting by installing curtains or venetian blinds. Direct sunlight will fade colors in painted or dyed materials, as well as in manuscripts. In a brightly lit room the exhibits appear drab and uninteresting, and brilliant reflections on the glass panels of the cases hide the displays behind them. The general illumination in exhibit rooms should be subdued. In so far as possible the cases should be so arranged as to eliminate the reflections caused by windows, overhead lights, or nearby lighted displays. A successful arrangement is to have the case interiors more strongly lighted than the room itself. This vitalizes the displays and attracts the observer, who seems to be looking out through a window at the materials shown. The light sources should be shielded from the observer and so placed as to avoid casting unnatural and distracting shadows and multiple shadows. Spot lights and flood lights may be used to accentuate special exhibits and objects within an exhibit. Because the lamps generate heat, the advisability of providing adequate ventilation should be examined. Fluorescent tubular lamps are well adapted for use in lighting case interiors. They use less power and create less heat than incandescent lamps. Care must be used in choosing the kind of fluorescent tube for use in an exhibit because some tend to alter the color values of the objects they illuminate.

A good exhibit program is one that is carefully planned, well organized, and attractively presented. To be successful as well it must be used and enjoyed by the visitors for whom it was constructed. A conscious effort must be made to furnish these guests of the museum with a restful environment in which they may feel at ease, undisturbed by distracting annoyances.

The frequent use of cardboard signs giving orders, such as "No Smoking," "Do Not Lean On Glass," "Please Do Not Touch," and "Quiet Please," distract attention from the exhibits and annoy visitors. A conspicuous ashtray placed beside the entrance to the exhibits, with the single word "Please" attached, should be a sufficient reminder for smokers. It is disconcerting to a visitor to find himself under the constant and apparently suspicious observation of an attendant as he moves from case to case. If the environment of the exhibits seems to require the use of these distracting petty admonitions and surveillances, then the environment needs to be changed.

The physical arrangement of the cases may be the source of several annoying inconveniences. If the aisles between cases are too narrow, a single individual studying a display will interfere with the freedom of movement of others. Insufficient space in front of a popular display that attracts groups of visitors will stop the movement of others or force an unnecessary detour. The resultant situation will resemble that in an overstocked and crowded supermarket. Dead-end galleries, which require the visitor to retrace his steps past a series of exhibits he has just seen, tend to break the continuity of his interest and lessen the enjoyment of the museum experience. Some visitors become annoyed when they find, after examining several displays, that they have been following them in reverse of the normal and recommended sequence.

These potential sources of visitor irritation indicate a need for studying visitor traffic patterns under both normal and crowded conditions before planning the distribution of the display cases in the exhibit rooms. They need not be arranged in straight lines and geometric patterns. They may be grouped to form alcoves along each side of a room. Adjacent cases may be placed at an angle to one another, as space requirements dictate. The cases may be arranged in an irregular pattern, creating a winding corridor lined with cases that serves as a one-way traffic route for the visitors. The application of some ingenuity and planning should eliminate most traffic hazards in exhibit rooms.

Continuous standing and strolling from display to display for a considerable length of time is a form of exercise to which many visitors are not accustomed and one that creates "museum fatigue." Tired feet and an aching back, physiological annoyances that greatly interfere with the visitor's enjoyment of the exhibits, can be avoided by offering opportunities for resting. Hard benches or a single chair placed in out-of-the-way corners are inadequate and tantalizing concessions to museum fatigue. Comfortable benches or davenports and groups of chairs invite visitors to rest, smoke, and visit together. In a small museum four modern Windsor chairs grouped around a small coffee table on which are ashtrays and a vase of flowers indicate an interest in visitor comfort. When the exhibits are extensive, resting areas should be provided in several sections of the exhibit rooms. In some parts of the country a soft drink vending machine is an indispensable piece of equipment, though not in the exhibit rooms. Obviously a conscious effort to extend full hospitality to the museum visitor will enhance the pleasure of his visit and lead him to encourage others to make similar visits.

And, of course, it is important that the visitors' toilets be clearly marked, easy of access, and relatively inconspicuous.

A museum is judged by its exhibits. The exhibit rooms are the show rooms in which the public is made aware of the role the museum can play in community life. The exhibit program is the most valuable and flexible interpretive instrument the institution possesses. Some of the principles and techniques that may be used in developing it have been discussed. Generally speaking, the quality of presentation is far more important than the quantity of time, energy, and funds expended upon its creation. A small group of coordinated and attractive exhibits will do a better job of interpretation than exhibits showing a greater number and variety of objects in poorly arranged displays.

The task of developing a satisfactory exhibit program is not a difficult one. The process is similar to that followed by a housewife, often assisted by an interior decorator, in making the rooms of her home comfortable and charming. It is analogous to those used by professional designers in creating the provocative displays in the larger stores. The primary objective is to establish in the mind of the visitor a sympathetic mood which will lead him to observe, enjoy, and understand the message the program seeks to convey. The continuity of exhibits and the organization of the individual displays will be achieved by exercising good taste and imaginative planning seasoned with ingenuity.

SUPPLEMENTARY SERVICES

The two most valuable ways to interpret the collections and the objectives of the museum are through the displays in the public exhibit halls and through the dissemination of knowledge derived from investigations of the materials in the collections. In order to realize the full potential of these two instruments the museum must offer a variety of supplementary services. Their purposes are to stimulate the citizens and visitors in the community to see the exhibits more frequently and make greater use of the specialized information the museum possesses.

The most rewarding and widely practiced of these services are those relating to the museum's work with the schools. It is obvious that the museum is an educational institution. It is not always sufficiently recognized as an important factor in the field of visual education. Usually the museum must initiate the establishment of an organized pattern of cooperation with the schools.

In some communities individual teachers bring classes to see the exhibits once or twice a year without solicitation from museum officials. The benefits received depend upon the teachers' attitudes. Such visits are commendable but are relatively ineffective because they do not take full advantage of the available instructional opportunities. They are apt to be considered sightseeing excursions unrelated to classroom interests.

Museum officials must actively promote closer relations with the schools. The axiom of good salesmanship applies here as well as elsewhere: discover the clients' interests and needs and then seek to meet them. Do not attempt to work through the teachers, for they rarely determine their own class schedules. Museum officials should discuss with the administrators responsible for the school curricula and schedules the ways and means by which the museum's exhibits can supplement existing classroom instruction. Once the school authorities realize that these museum facilities actually will illustrate and dramatize subjects taught in the classroom, it is merely a matter of time and negotiation before satisfactory arrangements are completed for closer integration between the two organizations.

The museum should be willing to make minor adjustments in its exhibit program in order to conform more closely to the school needs. It could schedule temporary exhibits of objects that are relevant to the subjects currently being studied in the school curriculum. The duration of each temporary exhibit would depend upon the number of days or weeks needed to enable all interested classes to see it. School authorities will normally attempt to adjust class schedules so that every class of one or more grades in every school in the community has the opportunity to visit the museum at least once during a school year; sometimes they will provide for several class periods at the museum. It has been found that children in the fourth, fifth, and sixth grades are most likely to obtain the greatest benefit from such visits. In order to avoid conflicts with other classes and to insure receiving the anticipated services, a teacher should reserve time on the museum's appointment calendar at least two weeks in advance of the visit.

The importance of the museum visit as a school assignment and the reasons for making it should be discussed in the classroom in advance. After the visit, a variety of devices may be used in the classroom to strengthen its impact and meaning in relation to the curriculum. Most classroom teachers find it difficult to adjust their teaching methods to the museum environment, to hold the pupils' attention, and to take full pedagogical advantage of the exhibits. For best instructional results the museum should furnish as guide a staff member or a qualified volunteer trained in the use of museum teaching methods. This museum teacher should be sufficiently familiar with the classroom studies of the visiting pupils to be able to relate the lessons learned in the museum to those being taught in the classroom.

Another means of cooperation is for the museum to carry its services to the school. Arrangements can be made for a museum staff member to give a talk, illustrated with objects from the collections, at the school assembly or in a classroom, upon a subject currently being studied. A similar service is rendered by making loans of small groups of articles from the collections to the schools for short periods for classroom use, or for display in glass cases in corridors. These temporary school loans are often accompanied by typewritten texts for the teachers' use.

A successful program of cooperation between the museum and the schools is one of the most satisfactory means of winning the good will of citizens of the community. The teachers and their administrators will recognize that the museum visits have increased pupil interest in the subjects being studied. Pupils will carry home their enthusiasm for the treasures seen at the museum and probably will insist upon serving as guides for their parents on an early return visit to the exhibit halls. A statistical analysis of the number of classes and pupils served during the school year may be a significant argument when the museum makes application to the city authorities for an appropriation to assist in the support of the services it renders to "the future citizens of the community."

The popularity of the exhibits can be increased by deliberate gestures of hospitality on the part of the museum management. Special guide service may be offered to interested groups, such as the Boy Scouts and Girl Scouts, the 4-H clubs, PTA chapters, and various study groups. Invitations may be issued to civic organizations to hold special meetings in the exhibit rooms at least once a year. Afternoon or evening receptions at which light refreshments are served may be arranged for the benefit of delegates to conventions, or to mark the opening of a new exhibit, or to celebrate some community anniversary or achievement. Such institutional hospitality demonstrates the interest of the museum in community activities and acquaints the guests with the nature of the exhibits.

A more formal expression of this hospitality calls for the establishment of a calendar of weekly or monthly organized meetings at the museum. For children there may be late afternoon or Saturday morning sessions for exhibit games, story-telling, model-making, or movies. Similar services may be offered adults in the late afternoons or in the evenings for meetings of study and hobby clubs, and for lectures, demonstrations, and documentary and travel movies.

It is important that all of these hospitable activities be related to the museum's objectives or fall within the framework of its interests. If they become too numerous and diversified, the museum may acquire the character of a community social center, which tends to obscure its functions and destroy the dignity of its standing in the community.

Another rewarding supplementary service a museum may render is the lending of materials from the collections to other community organizations that install exhibits from time to time as a public service. Among these are banks, stores, hotels, libraries, hospitals, and chambers of commerce. These exhibits may be a continuous series of changing displays or short-term ones for conventions, anniversaries, and special events, or at county fairs. By assisting in the creation of these exhibits the museum broadens its exhibit program, receives wider recognition through the card of acknowledgment of the loan in each extra-mural display, and gains civic credit for rendering a useful service to community organizations. The conditions surrounding the loaned materials will differ with each borrower. Before undertaking this supplementary service the museum should formulate policies defining the acceptable types of borrowing organizations, stating the conditions under which the loaned objects may be used and displayed, and stipulating the security and insurance measures that need to be guaranteed by the borrower. Most museums do not permit the loan of materials from their collections to private individuals for display or entertainment purposes.

Several supplementary services are the inevitable by-products of the technical knowledge and professional competence of the members of the museum staff. One of the most important of these is guidance and help to visitors who request additional information upon subjects dealt with in the exhibits. Printed or mimeographed leaflets and bibliographies may often supply the answers. Yet every staff member should be willing, when asked, to take time to discuss a subject with an inquirer, offer advice and assistance, and encourage further studies.

Another one of this group of services is lecturing to various local organizations, usually during the off-duty time of the lecturer. When the lecture, illustrated with slides or objects from the collections, is about the museum and its purposes or upon a subject in which the museum is interested, no fee should be charged, for it is a legitimate museum service. It is one of the best means of creating a wider interest in the museum within the community. In this activity, as in the case of making short-term loans, rules should be made governing the circumstances under which invitations to speak will be accepted. Otherwise the speaker will find himself swamped with lecture engagements of doubtful value for which he cannot charge a fee.

A third service in this category calls for giving an authoritative statement on the origin and use of some privately owned object brought to the museum for identification. The courteous act of sharing knowledge with another will bring credit to the museum, for the owner expects to receive an authoritative statement from the museum, not the private opinion of an individual. Many such requests can be answered quickly and easily. Others will require comparison with similar materials and consultation of technical references. An opinion should not be rendered until these investigations are completed. If an object defies accurate identification because of lack of knowledge or facilities, it is wise to admit failure frankly and suggest some other source from which the identification may be obtained. To employ guesswork or impressive technical terms to hide an unsatisfactory identification jeopardizes the good name of the museum. Under no circumstances should the museum place a monetary value upon any article brought in for identification or evaluation. A museum cannot afford to be quoted officially as having placed a financial value upon any privately owned article. In the dealers' market the price of an historic object is determined by the immediate pressures of supply and demand on the part of both the buyer and the seller.

A closely related service involves giving advice and help in the care and preservation of privately owned materials similar to those in the museum's collections. For example, a member of the governing board has a portrait that should be cleaned. Or the wife of an old friend wishes to know how to prevent silver from tarnishing, or the best way to clean fragile old textiles. Perhaps the problem is the repair of a prized broken porcelain vase. The answer should be given if the desired knowledge is available. The inquirer may be referred to someone better qualified to supply the desired information. In the name of the museum as a public institution a conscientious effort should be made to supply the guidance sought.

The supplementary interpretive services small history museums can render are many and varied. A single museum may not find it practical to offer all of these discussed here. Yet its officials should be able to determine the degree to which it is taking advantage of its potentials in this field and the extent to which it must make adjustments in order to improve its existing supplementary services.

The Social Significance

The preceding pages contain many suggestions and recommendations and some instructions on how to carry out essential museum procedures. Many a reader may feel overwhelmed and frustrated by the discovery that the management of a small history museum is apparently such a complicated undertaking. Actually this bulletin is a synoptic review of basic museum practices worked out by a great many people who have sought through several generations to improve the usefulness of museums as social instruments. An effort has been made to maintain an obvious continuity of presentation that demonstrates the relationships of the subjects discussed, and at the same time to emphasize the essential simplicity of museum objectives. It is hoped that these closing paragraphs will reassure those who falter and stimulate those who are confident.

The key to the museum movement is to be found in the existence of things that play a role in the intellectual life of our society. The history museum is the only community institution dedicated to protecting historical things, other than library and archival materials, from loss or destruction in order that they may be enjoyed and studied by the present and future generations of citizens. If these things are worth keeping as historical source materials, the identity of each item must be guarded. Time and energy are required to keep accurate records and to care for the collections, which are the museum's principal assets. The only reason for preserving collections is to use them as a means of bringing pleasure and knowledge to as many people as possible. To do this they must be publicly exhibited and interpreted. Considerable planning and studying should be done to create attractive and informative exhibits, which make a visit to the museum seem worthwhile. But even then the job is not quite done. In order to play an active part in the life of the community, the museum should offer supplementary services that will encourage more frequent use of the exhibits and aid in the pursuit of new interests created by them. The philosophy of good museum management is just that simple.

Yet a well organized museum may fail to achieve its objectives if it exists in a civic and social vacuum, out of touch with the daily interests and preoccupations of the community it seeks to serve. Constructive and occasionally aggressive steps must be taken to achieve the dignity and respect to which all public service agencies are entitled and to win the good will and support of the citizens and organizations of the community. It should be well known that the pattern of museum administration conforms with generally accepted principles of good institutional management and of sound fiscal policy. The various elements in the community should be kept in close touch with the museum and its work through a continuous and dignified program of publicity carried in museum newsletters, in newspapers and regional magazines, and on radio and television.

The local history museum has the unique privilege and responsibility of serving as the tangible expression of the living memory of the community by giving its citizens the opportunity to see and understand the objects that once played a part in its past experiences. A first-hand vivid contact with former events contributes to a better understanding of the origins and growth of present community interests and activities and may modify public attitudes toward current civic problems. The dual functions of the museum make it potentially capable of becoming an important and influential public service institution.

Every museum is a unit in the growing national museum movement. A survey conducted in 1966 by the U.S. Office of Education revealed that at that time there were 2,889 museums in the

United States. Approximately fifty per cent of them were listed as history museums. Many changes have occurred since that survey. Some museums have ceased to exist. Many new museums have been established. The movement generally has been strengthened and broadened. It is evident that there are more museums in this country today than there were eight years ago, and it may be safely assumed that *at least* one-half of them concentrate their interests upon historical subjects.

The leading museums of the country have achieved the status of influential and indispensable community institutions. Every museum faces the challenge of attaining a similar respected position within its own sphere of influence. It may come to pass that in another generation, near the close of the twentieth century, community museums, the majority of which will deal with local history, will play as important a role in the cultural life of the communities they serve as do public libraries today. The realization of this prophecy depends upon the extent to which local history museums carry out their obligations as educational and cultural public service agencies.

Every museum is a link in the chain that gives unity to the national museum movement. Regardless of its individuality, its special interests, or its regional character, it is linked to other museums by objectives that are common to all. In every community the strength of this chain is judged by the character of the link with which its citizens are familiar. The strength of each link lies not in its size but in the success with which it approximates the ideal performance of its dual functions. No link in the chain, no single museum, stands alone. Through its inability to attain its objectives with reasonable success it weakens the entire chain. Through its contacts with sister institutions it strengthens the general museum movement and gains internal strength by doing so. In recognition of this interdependence, the officials of the stronger museums assist the weaker ones whenever they can. For the same reason firmer bonds are being established between museums with similar interests and between those located in each of the several regions of the country.

This document is designed as an instrument to help forge stronger links in this unifying chain of the museum movement. It will serve its purpose best if, in addition to furnishing guidance, it stimulates discussion of management practices between museums through personal visits or by correspondence. The eagerness with which museum staff members welcome an opportunity to compare experiences and discuss problems of mutual interest with colleagues is one of the heart-warming attributes of the national museum movement. One valuable source of guidance and advice on museum matters is the American Association of Museums, Suite 428, 1055 Thomas Jefferson Street, N. W., Washington, D.C. 20007. Another source is the American Association for State and Local History, 1400 Eighth Avenue South, Nashville, Tennessee, 37203, the publisher of this booklet.

Those who desire additional information upon the subjects relating to museum management may find what they seek in one or another of the following publications. The book by Laurence Vail Coleman is out of print but may be consulted in most public and museum libraries.

Alexander, Edward P. *Museums in Motion* (title tentative). Nashville: AASLH, 1978.

Burcaw, G. Ellis. *Introduction to Museum Work.* Nashville: AASLH, 1975

Coleman, Laurence Vail. *Manual for Small Museums.* New York: G.P. Putnam's, 1927. (Out of print)

Dudley, Dorothy H., and Irma B. Wilkinson. *Museum Registration Methods,* 3rd ed. Washington, D.C.: American Association of Museums, 1977.

Guldbeck, Per E. *Care of Historical Collections.* Nashville: AASLH, 1972.

Guthe, Carl E. *So You Want A Good Museum.* Boulder, Colo.: Pruett Press, 1969. (Out of print)

Long, Charles J. *Museums Workers Notebook.* San Antonio, Texas: Witte Museum, 1957.

Neal, Arminta. *Exhibits for the Small Museum.* Nashville: AASLH, 1976.

Neal, Arminta. *Help! for the Small Museum.* Boulder, Colo.: Pruett Press, 1969.

Parker, Arthur C. *A Manual for History Museums.* New York: Columbia University Press, 1935.

Rath, Frederick L., and Merrilyn Rogers O'Connell. *A Bibliography on Historical Organization Practices.* Nashville: AASLH,

1975–. Volume 1: Historic Preservation. Volume 2: Care and Conservation of Collections. Volume 3: Interpretation.

Russell, Charles. *Museums and Our Children.* New York: Central Book Co., 1956.

Stowell, Alice M. *The Living Museum.* New York: Vantage Press, 1956.

Tilden, Freeman. *Interpreting Our Heritage,* 2nd ed. Nashville: AASLH, 1967.

An Invitation

The American Association for State and Local History, founded in 1940, is a nonprofit educational organization dedicated to advancing knowledge, understanding, and appreciation of localized history in the United States and Canada. It serves amateur and professional historians, individuals and organizations, and includes in its broad spectrum such groups as historical museums and libraries, junior history clubs, historic sites, manuscript collections, and large as well as small historical societies.

To encourage the development of popular knowledge about American history, the Association launched the magazine *American Heritage* in 1949. Within five years it became a bimonthly, hardcover magazine published professionally by American Heritage Publishing Company and cosponsored by the Association. Royalties help provide some of the financial resources needed to carry out the Association's broad educational and professional programs. In recent years, the National Endowment for the Humanities, the National Endowment for the Arts, the Council on Library Resources, and the National Museum Act have provided funds to the Association to support special training programs, seminars for historical agency personnel, consultant services, and publications.

Membership in the Association is open to professionals, institutions, libraries, and individuals.

PROFESSIONAL SERVICES: Clearinghouse for inquiries from individuals and organizations; cassette lectures and slide/tape training kits; research surveys about the profession; job placement service; consultant service to historical societies and museums; annual awards of merit and commendation for outstanding contributions to the field by individuals and organizations; cooperative programs with state and regional conferences of historical organizations; annual meeting; joint meetings with related historical organizations.

PUBLICATIONS: *History News,* monthly magazine of up-to-date news of members, events, new ideas, reviews of books, and a Technical Leaflet series of how-to-do-it articles (with a 3-ring binder available); *Directory of Historical Societies* and *Agencies in the United States and Canada,* biennial; books and booklets; job placement newsletter, quarterly; *Newsletter,* occasional, special issues on matters of urgent importance; catalog of Association publications and technical leaflets; catalog of slide/tape training kits and cassette lectures. *History News* and out-of-print volumes of Association *Bulletins,* a series of booklets published between 1941 and 1973 which preceded the Technical Leaflet series, are available in microfilm from Xerox University Microfilms, 300 N. Zeeb Road, Ann Arbor, Michigan 48106.

TRAINING PROGRAMS: Cosponsor of annual Williamsburg Seminar for Historical Administrators; seminars on publications, administration of historical agencies and museums, historical museum techniques, management and interpretation of history museums and historic sites; training seminars and regional workshops for beginning professionals and small agency directors.

For further information on the Association, its membership benefits, and its extensive list of publications for the profession, please write:

> The Director
> American Association for State and Local History
> 1400 Eighth Avenue South
> Nashville, Tennessee 37203